LESSONS FROM
A LIFETIME OF
Love and Loss

LESSONS FROM A LIFETIME OF

Love and Loss

Reflections and Stories from a Mother of Eight

ERICA ANDERSON

Printed in the United States of America
Published in Hellertown, PA

Cover design by Kim Lewis

Library of Congress number 2025902296
ISBN 979-8-89420-038-5

For more information or to place bulk orders, contact the author or the publisher at Jennifer@BrightCommunications.net.

Bright
COMMUNICATIONS

To my children and grandchildren: We have not always agreed. The reason that I have not given up is because of each of you. I love every one of you! To my mama, thank you for never giving up on me although I was so rebellious. To my grandad, Henry Burch Sr., thanks for introducing me to Jesus! To my grandma Callie Mae, thank you for rescuing me from those streets when I was most vulnerable!

"For God so loved the world that He gave His only begotten son, that whosoever believeth him should not perish, but have everlasting life."
—John 3:16

Me and five of my grandchildren

Contents

Introduction: A Time to Heal

"This is what it means to trust God: We will be sure about the things that we hope for. We will be sure in our minds about things that we cannot even see."
—*Hebrews 11:1 (Easy Bible)*

SURE = *adjective*
confident in what one thinks or knows; having no doubt that one is right.

"I'm sure that my name is Erica."

Often in life, people attempt to define *your* life—from their own minimal knowledge of what they think that they know about you!

But they have not endured your circumstances. They have not walked in your shoes. They might have been around you, but they are *not* you. After much consideration and years, I have concluded that no one can tell my life story like I can. Even if you have had similar experiences to mine, our outcomes will be different, and our perceptions of those outcomes will be unique.

In this book, I discuss all that I have survived, from my childhood raised as an only child by my alcoholic mother, with my crack-addicted father making guest appearances now and then, through my teen years that were filled with me running away from home, suicide attempts, sex, drinking, and smoking marijuana. I will share how I was thrust into early adulthood by my father who encouraged me to drop out of high school so that he could stop paying child support. When I began having children at the tender age of fifteen, I vowed that I would be a better parent than mine had been.

Even though I did not always hit that mark, I am extremely proud that I raised my children with the Lord front and center and forming the foundation of our lives. I emphasized the importance of education, and I stressed that my job as their mother was to raise my children to be productive members of society. I am proud that the first six of my eight children have graduated high school, and so far, two of my children have/are attending college. I am immensely proud of my children.

Dear reader, I hope my story gives you insight into your own, and I hope you gain confidence in your ability to change the trajectory of your life. Your starting point does not determine your ending.

I call my book a Springboard Story because as you read my story, you'll see shaded sections of questions and lines for you to write *your* story. Please allow my story to spring your own. I hope and believe that you writing *your* story will be as healing and transforming for *you* as writing my story was so healing and transforming for *me*.

Our capacity for growth is determined by how open our minds are to learning about ourselves and to improving our responses to challenging people and circumstances. When the chips are down and the emotions are high, can you preserve your peace?

I know that I have come a long way, yet I am nowhere near where I am destined to be. Writing this book has been therapeutic for me. It enabled me to reflect upon my progress and to dream about my future. I am excited about the next phase of my life—and the next, and the next!

I hope to leave a positive impact on the people I encounter in this life—including you! I hope to encourage you and lift you up. As you use the prompts in this book as a springboard to share *your* story, I hope you too reflect upon your progress and dream about your future.

If I can make it through the hell that I have endured, I am certain that there is hope for you! I believe in you!

What are some of your big dreams?

_____

_____

_____

_____

_____

_____

_____

_____

_____

_____

What are the biggest challenges you have overcome?

_____

_____

_____

_____

_____

_____

_____

_____

_____

_____

_____

How might sharing your story inspire other people?

_____

_____

_____

_____

_____

_____

_____

_____

_____

_____

_____

_____

_____

_____

_____

_____

_____

_____

"If God gives such attention to the appearance of wildflowers—most of which are never even seen—don't you think he will attend to you, take pride in you, do his best for you? What I am trying to do here is to get you to relax, to not be so preoccupied with getting, so you can respond to God's giving. People who do not know God and the way He works fuss over these things, but you know both God and how He works. Steep your life in God-reality, God-initiative, God-provisions. Do not worry about missing out. You will find all your everyday human concerns will be met."
—Matthew 6:30-33 (Message Bible)

My parents and me

Chapter 1: You Are Not Your Past

"God blessed them and said to them, 'Be fruitful and increase in number, fill the earth and subdue it. Rule over the fish in the sea and the birds in the sky and over every living creature that moves on the ground.'"
—Genesis 1:28 (NIV Bible)

My Timeline

Born: January 9, 1979, at 12:17 pm to Paul D. Anderson and Linda R. Burch

Ages 5 to 10: Childhood traumas: witness of domestic violence, attempt of molestation by a family friend

Age 12: Ran away from home

Age 13: Attempted molestation by Mama's boyfriend

Age 14: First abortion and suicide attempt: I took several of Grandad's pills. It only made me sick.

Age 15: Gave birth to Camisha in November 1994

Age 17: Got a job at the Jewish Orthodox in dietary, then became a State-Tested Nurse Assistant, had an abortion

Age 18: Moved into my first apartment

Age 19: Gave birth to the twins, Serenity and Gregory, in February 1998

Age 20: Had another abortion and was running the streets smoking weed, drinking, and partying was suicidal

Age 21: Gave birth to Eric in September 2000

Age 23: My mama died on May 19, 2002. On October 24, 2002, I purchased my first home.

Age 25: Gave birth to Arabia in August 2004. On December 11, 2004, I got married.

Age 27: Gave birth to DJ in April 2006

Age 28: Had a miscarriage

Age 29: Gave birth to Amoz in June 2008

Age 32: Gave birth to Joshua in December 2010

Age 33: My daddy died.

Age 34: Became a nurse (LPN)

Age 36: Became an Ordained Minister

Age 39: Baptized my baby boy at Christ Emmanuel

Age 41: Divorced

Age 42: Relocated to North Carolina

What is your timeline?

_____

_____

_____

_____

_____

_____

_____

_____

_____

_____

_____

_____

_____

Erica Anderson

As I sat to begin my first chapter, after reflecting on a general timeline of my life, I realized that I have come so extremely far. I am not who I was in the past.

Many things occurred in my life that I did not choose, but I also made plenty of my own choices. I could attempt to shift blame for the challenges I have faced onto my parents; however, something inside of me will not allow me to be in victim mode.

I feel a profound energy pushing me into the next phase of my life! This energy keeps me grounded, prevents me from comparing my life to others, and encourages me to embrace the next milestones. I am certain of one thing: God has been with me this entire time.

I know that I am nowhere near where I am destined to be, but I am far from my starting point. Along my journey, I was given a picture of the Spirit of the living God carrying a woman over violent waves of the ocean. If you have ever been to the beach, you have seen how ferocious those waters can be! Sometimes in my life, I have faced violent situations, and yet God carried me— and He still does. Based on Deuteronomy 31:8, "The Lord himself goes before you and will be with you; He will never leave you nor forsake you." Through all the heartache and pain, the losses and betrayals, and the mental and verbal abuse I endured, God remained consistently available to me.

This is my story.

Writing about my life has opened up some old wounds that I have sustained over the years. The process has been quite painful, yet it's also healing when I recall how far I have come in just 46 years of life. I hope that you can read what I have gone and grown through as encouragement to know that you too can make it through any challenge that you will ever be faced with in this life. My life has been full of many twists and turns, nevertheless I did not give up. I am still here to tell my story.

"You are my hiding place; you will protect me from trouble and surround me with songs of deliverance."
—Psalm 32:7 (NIV)

Let me be clear: I am not shifting blame on my mother for anything; however, my childhood was the crucible for all my future challenges. Fortunately, I have used my circumstances as steppingstones to elevate myself to my God-given purpose!

My mother raised me the best way she knew how. She did what she could, and time and experience gave me the grace to forgive her—although it took me 20 years after my mother's death. I am so grateful that I have done so. Finding forgiveness allowed me to share my story, hoping that other people can learn from it and make better choices in their lives.

I was told that when my mama, "Net," was pregnant with me, she was drinking and partying too much, so my granddad made her stay in the house until she gave birth. Within a week of Granddad's demand, I was born.

I was told my hair was so nappy as a baby that one of my cousins said, "Somebody needs to get that baby a perm." For a long time, I hated my thick, wavy-at-the-roots hair. I internalized the lies that I was told that I had unkempt hair from birth. It is ironic that today most of my family members who criticized my hair are either bald, wear wigs or hair weaves, or are no longer here to tell the story.

For all appearances, I was raised in a good Christian home. Our family even went to church together every Sunday.

But behind closed doors, the soundtrack of our home was loud arguing, fussing, and cussing. Some family fights even brought out the big guns—literally.

My mama was at the center of every brawl. When she drank, she said what was on her mind, especially concerning our family's dysfunction. Mama epitomized the old saying, "A drunk doesn't tell no lies."

Despite my mama's volatility, she had a giving heart. She would give anyone the best and the least of anything she had. Yet she was not appreciated or respected—not even by me.

As I grew up, I often heard how bad off Net was because of her drinking. But it was more than hearsay: I had hard evidence.

My mama would come to my school, St. Mark, extremely drunk. One afternoon, she was so drunk that she slid right off a bench to the floor in the school hallway.

A teacher who was also a family friend told her, "Get up and get yourself together!"

My mama listened to her; she knew that teacher did not play any games!

One of my most embarrassing moments was at a parents' volleyball game. The parents were out on the court, and the spectators in the stands cheered, having so much fun—except me. I was ready to go home because I could feel in my bones something bad was about to happen.

And oh yes, it did. Midway through the game, my mama fell flat on her face, and her dentures flew out of her mouth and slid across the volleyball court.

I shrank down in my seat, wishing that I could just disappear.

One of my classmates turned and asked, "Isn't that your mother?"

"It's not my fault," I mumbled, embarrassed. Even as a young child, I knew that someone else's actions were not my responsibility. For a long while after that, my mama was the talk of the school, among the parents and the students alike.

Some things that my mama did caused me to get bullied at school. I used to get chased home by one girl who taunted me, "Wasn't that your mama?" She relentlessly reminded me—and everyone else—about my mom's falling in the gym that day.

One day, one of my friends told me, "You aren't about to get chased home one more day!" She and her older brother reassured me that they had my back. That day, I fought back, and the tables turned. I went from being bullied, to *being* the bully. I did not just bully my tormentor; I bullied a lot of other girls. I used to make one of the girls carry my books, and I took another girl's lunch and money, especially her pretzels. They were one of my favorites.

As I became an adult, I prayed to God to forgive me and to send the girls I had bullied to me so that I could apologize. Years later, He did just that. I saw one of the girls on the bus. I tried to talk to her, but she pretended she did not know me. Years later, I ran into another one of the girls in a grocery store. When I apologized to her, she said that she did not remember any of it.

Today I absolutely despise bullying. I realized that the bully needs help too. When I was being bullied, I was miserable, and I wanted to inflict the same pain upon someone else. I just could not be in that nightmare all alone.

In addition to acting out bullying, growing up I also suppressed a lot of my memories and emotions of pain, disappointment, and uncertainties. I was never able to anticipate what was coming next. I desperately wanted to escape the nightmare that I was currently living in.

Growing up, my mama's drunken behavior was compounded by domestic violence. I recall four major incidents. The first happened late one night when I was around five years old. My mama's boyfriend, Miguel, picked my mama and me up from my paternal grandparents' home in College Hill in Ohio. As Miguel was driving, he was upset with my mama about something. Miguel pulled over on Gray Road, which is dark, winding, and dangerous—the scene of many car accident fatalities.

"Get out!" Miguel commanded my mom. Then he turned to me and said, "You! Stay in here!"

Even as a little girl, I was determined to protect my mama. I got out of the car with her, and Miguel angrily sped off into the night.

A few minutes later, God sent a car to us with some young White people in it and one light-skinned Black man. They stopped and asked if we needed help, then they drove us from College Hill back to our apartment in Evanston. Unfortunately, even after we arrived home, the nightmare was far from over. My mama had secured the front door with the chain, but when Miguel showed up, he kicked the door in like a ravaging beast!

Once Miguel was in the apartment, he commenced whooping my mama's butt. As I watched, he hit her so hard he broke her jaw. While Miguel beat my mama, he hit me too.

I ran to the phone to call for help. Those were the days before 911; we dialed 0 to reach the police. I knew that Granddad would get to us before the police would, so I called him instead. He had wisely taught me how to dial his number when I was about four years old.

As I was desperately trying to call for help, my mama crazily tried to stop me! I did not care, and I did not stop because I knew that I did not deserve to be exposed to that kind of mess. I was calling for help—whether she wanted me to or not.

When my granddad arrived, he punched Miguel so hard it broke *his* jaw. Both Miguel and my mama went to the hospital and had their jaws wired shut. Miguel did not come around much after that!

The second domestic violence situation I recall involved my mama's next boyfriend, Jack. One night when I was about eight years old, my mama and I were visiting Jack and his family, and a major fight erupted between Jack and my mama. Jack forced my mama to hang out of a second-story window as if he was going to throw her out. I ran to the kitchen, grabbed a knife, and put it on his back.

Jack's son begged me, "Don't stab my daddy."

"Your daddy had better let my mama back into that window, or your daddy is going out that window with her," I said, still pressing the knife to his dad's back.

Hearing me, Jack eased up on my mama and let her back into the room. It helped that I had made a deep impression on his back with that knife.

The third violent episode was with my mama's new boyfriend, Authur. This man got three strikes against him! The first time, when I was around nine years old, Arthur, my mama, and I were driving in her car. Suddenly, he grabbed a ring that he had given to my mama right off her hand. He slid it onto his finger, then punched her in the face it. Her blood spurted everywhere.

I was so angry that I ripped the rearview mirror right off my mama's Audi, and I tried with all my little might to fight that man and hit him with the mirror. He thrust out his arm to my forehead to put space in between us. From that moment on, I hated him.

The second time, Authur busted my mama's head to the white meat with a baseball bat. Thankfully, I did not see it happen, but seeing my mama's head split open was just as damaging. After that, Jack took my mama to the hospital to get her head stitched up.

I despised Arthur. I had a Jem's doll poster hanging up in my grandparents' kitchen. One day, I told my cousins to come into the kitchen to watch something. When they came into the kitchen, I began to throw knives at the poster. Instead of Jem's doll, I had visions of Authur, and every knife that I threw stuck into his body.

After throwing knives at the kitchen wall, I ran from the kitchen to the living room and began stabbing the middle of the couch, where my two cousins had gone back to watching TV. They quickly split apart in shock! There were no adults around to see or help. Our granddad was upstairs, but he didn't know what I was enduring at the time. This was the first nervous breakdown that I had.

Even after that, my mama continued to see Authur. I could not understand why. What did she see in that man? I feared Authur would kill my mama one day. My hatred of Authur evolved into hating *her* for allowing the abuse to happen. A few years later, when I was about thirteen years old, that same bastard tried to molest me. I will get back to that a little later in this book.

But that was not the first time I faced sexual abuse. One day, I was at a motorcycle club on Montgomery Road, next to a hair salon, with my mama. I was wearing my favorite Chicago Bulls starter coat. It was so big that it hung to my knees. It was all black with the Bull's face on the back. I was a huge Michael Jordan fan, and I loved that coat!

Back then, my mama was spending time with a family associate—a creepy old man. She had gone into the back room in the club. I was in the front room of the club playing on a Ping-

Pong machine. Out of nowhere, the creepy old man came over to me and stood close. Then he began running his hand across my chest. My breasts were just starting to develop.

I do not remember him saying anything. I only remember how afraid I was. But I also felt empowered because I could not wait to get home to tell my granddad, who I knew would take care of it.

Unlike many little girls and boys who are molested and afraid to tell anyone because they have been manipulated by the perpetrator into thinking that it is their fault, I knew that it was *not* my fault. Hear me now: *It is not your fault!*

Just then, my mama came out of the back room toward me.

"Please can we go?" I begged her. I did not tell her what had happened because I knew in my heart that she could not help me.

And I was right. My mama could barely help *herself,* let alone me. As Mama and I walked back to my grandparents' house, she was stumbling and staggering behind me. I began to run as fast as I could to get to my granddad because I wanted to tell him what had happened to me before my mama got into the house.

When I told Granddad, he became enraged. He was fiercely protective of me, with the belief: *"If someone is messing with you, they are messing with me!"* I internalized that protective nature later toward my own children.

Shortly after, when my mama stumbled into the door, Granddad snatched her up like a Raggedy Ann doll. Mama sobered up quick! Granddad grabbed his shotgun and threw it over his shoulder—I imagine like he had done back in World War II. We all piled into his black Pontiac two-door sedan, and he raced to the motorcycle club.

I could feel the anger coming from my mama. I knew she was mad at me, but I didn't care. She knew better than to say something to me because Granddad would have split her wig over me. He was my grandfather *and* my father, all rolled into one!

When we got inside the motorcycle club, I stood behind Granddad because I was afraid of the creepy old man who had touched me.

"Stand next to me," Granddad said, with his shotgun thrown back over his shoulder. Then he turned to the creepy old man and said, "If you ever look at my granddaughter again, let alone touch her or talk to her, I will blow your brains out!"

One thing was for sure: That creepy old man knew that my granddad would do just that.

Sure, thing, years later, I came across that same creepy old man at a function at his family's house. My family and his family were close, and they used to hang out. When the creepy old man recognized me, he dropped his head and stared at the floor. I bet that he remembered what my granddad said, and I bet that he knew my granddad would *still* make good on that promise!

Think of your life as chapters in your book. Sometimes they can be organized into places you've lived or schools you attended and jobs you've had. What do you remember about your elementary school days?

_____

_____

_____

_____

_____

_____

_____

_____

How did those events shape you?

_____

_____

_____

_____

_____

_____

_____

_____

Who from your childhood was a force for good? How did your relationship with them shape your future—as an adult and perhaps as a parent?

_____

_____

_____

_____

_____

_____

_____

_____

_____

_____

_____

_____

_____

_____

_____

_____

_____

_____

_____

_____

Erica Anderson

One of the many positive things my granddad did for me was he made sure that I knew the Lord and that I was well acquainted with the Bible. When I look back over my life, I know that God has always had His hands on me, and He continues to do so. Even as a little girl, I had such a love for Jesus!

It was a good thing the Lord was continuously watching over me because my mama certainly wasn't! When I was growing up, she often passed out drunk while I was in her care. My mama's sister, my Aunt Rosette, was always there for me when my mama was too drunk to even stand or see straight.

Mama and I lived upstairs from Aunt Rosette. Many evenings, I would stand in front of Aunt Rosette's door, waiting on her to get home from work. She was my escape. Not surprisingly, my mama did not like our relationship, probably because she feared that Aunt Rosette was taking me away from her. But what my mama did not realize was that Aunt Rosette was also my peace. Although as a child I did not know what peace was, I recognized that things were different when I was with Aunt Rosette instead of with my mama. With Aunt Rosette, I was able to just be a child, and I did not have to be tormented.

What do you remember from your middle school days?

_____

_____

_____

_____

How did those events shape you?

_____

_____

_____

_____

Has anyone in your life ever brought you peace?

_____

_____

_____

_____

_____

When you look back over your life, were there times when things should have ended in tragedy but instead things worked out on your behalf for good?

_____

_____

_____

_____

_____

Can you make any connections between those events? Do those events have anything in common?

_____

_____

_____

_____

_____

_____

Me as a teenager

Chapter 2: Broken Vessel

"I am forgotten as though I were dead;
I have become like broken pottery."
—Psalm 31:12 (NIV Bible)"

When I was about twelve years of age, I hit the age of account-ability. Yes, I knew right from wrong. But during that season of my life, wrong looked like right to me.

No one could tell me anything. "Rebellion" was my middle name, instead of Renee, which means "born again." I was an-gry, confused, and struggling with puberty hormonal changes. I wanted what I wanted when I wanted it, and no one was going to tell me anything different.

While I was in that state of disobedience, I was unaware that a hurricane was heading straight at me. At the tender age of twelve, I thought that I was in love. I craved love because my mama and daddy were far too busy with their own dysfunctions to give me even a fraction of the nurturing, time, attention, and love that I required—and deserved.

So I sought out things that appealed to my puberty-hor-mone-addled teen mind. One summer day while I was spending time at one of my aunt's houses, I met a boy who I thought that I liked and who I thought liked me.

But what did I know about relationships? Nothing really. I saw my mama with her boyfriends, and none of those clowns were worth anything. They all were disrespectful to my mama and me. None of them hesitated to beat her in front of me. I promised myself that no man was ever going to put his hands on me. I meant that, although I have experienced domestic violence, which I will discuss in later chapters.

Now back to this so-called love thing. I thought that I was so in love that I ran away from home. Before I ran away from home for the first time, I always felt that I was being held hostage by my grandparents, who literally didn't want me to leave their front porch. Yet, when it was convenient for my grandma, mama, and aunt, they dragged me to Perkins Bar on Montgomery Road so they could have a few drinks—even when I was as young as five years old. I had to sit in a booth by myself because I was not allowed to sit at the bar.

"Sit down. Have a hot pickle and a soda," Mama would command. Never heard of hot dill pickles? They are very common in Cincinnati, Ohio. I really loved hot pickles—still do. But even as a child, I knew Mama only bought me one to keep me quiet.

We went to that bar so often that I learned how to dance there—at age five. Crazy, right?

Other than those escapades, my grandparents wouldn't allow me to associate with the neighborhood kids because they said that those kids were bad. My mama was friendly with a few of the families, so I did get to be around some of the other kids when I was with her, but my granddad despised those actions. He could not stand the idea of me being exposed to so much.

I did not understand it back then, but now I understand my granddad was trying to protect me. But as a kid, I felt like I was in prison, and I desperately wanted to break free. One day when I was eleven years old and I was living with my grandparents, I was getting ready for school and I packed a big garbage bag full of clothes.

"Hey, Erica! What are you doing with that bag? What's in there?" Granddad asked.

"I'm giving these clothes that I can't fit to one of the kids at my school, Granddad," I lied.

"Erica, are you sure that you're not running away?" Granddad asked.

"Yes, I'm sure," I lied again. I hated that I lied to my granddad.

Needless to say, Granddad did not allow me to take those clothes to school, which at first threw a monkey-wrench into my plans. But I did not allow that to stop me. I still ran away.

When I was eleven-and-a-half years old, I ran away from home often, for weeks or months at a time for almost a year off and on. One time when I had been gone for quite a while, my family contacted the news. Cincinnati Channel 5 WLWT news anchor Curtis Fuller did a story on me. That was surprising because generally, they don't air news about runaway children—especially not runaway *Black* children.

At that time, I was gone for almost a month, although it felt like an entire year because I experienced so much torment. God surely was protecting me then. Without God's presence, I could not have made it!

I recall one Sunday when I had run away, I was sitting on the stairs of Christ Emmanuel Christian Fellowship Church in Cincinnati, Ohio, on May Street. The congregation was praising God so fervently it was vibrating the concrete steps on which I was sitting! I felt safe on those steps. I felt peace. I remember having the desire to go home, but Satan lied and told me that would not be a good idea. I will disclose in later chapters how God sent me back to Christ Emmanuel Christian Fellowship Church years later!

When I was out there on the streets all alone at twelve years old, I was treated like trash. Many demons planned my demise. I witnessed women getting high on crack cocaine in front of their babies. I noticed that many of their babies had effects that seemed like they had urges to get high. Back in 1992, one of the women who was heavy on crack called me into her bedroom. She closed the door.

"Sit down," she said.

I sat across the dark room from her. The only light was from the lighter when she lit up her crack pipe. She didn't say anything, but I saw the devil in her spirit. Satan thought that I would bite the bait. I was shocked and afraid.

Why'd she call me in the room with her, I wondered. *I bet she wants me to inquire about what she's doing, hoping I'll join her.* But God had a different plan for me.

I later found out that my so-called boyfriend, Jay, did not love me! I was devastated because I thought he was the one and because I was able to spend so much time with him, and he gained access to my innocent goods—my virginity. Unlike me, Jay did not have to run away. He had access to the streets; that is what he was used to. Suddenly, I was exposed to his way of living—life with no boundaries. His mother was dipping and dabbing in drugs, and his father was absent. I thought that was freedom, but the trap that I had fallen into was full of death, hell, and destructive behaviors. Jay and I did not live together; we went from house to house—on a road to nowhere.

One day, Jay left me in downtown Over-the-Rhine, Cincinnati. It was so scary!

Miraculously, when I was walking outside, I saw a family friend across the street at a bus stop. I ran over to speak to him. I so badly wanted to ask him for bus fare so I could go back home, but I was embarrassed. My pride would not allow me to.

I didn't know what was going to happen to me. I was left with a grown man named Nathan, who I later found out was almost thirty years old. Nathan took me to the back of his store. His place was damp, dark—unlike anything I was used to. It was not a place of safety for a young child, such as I was at the time.

Even back then, I knew that Nathan intended to sexually abuse me. When he touched me in between my legs, I remember praying, *God, please protect me.* I no longer wanted to be a runaway. I wanted to be home. Deep down, I knew that my life was in danger.

Not long after, one of Nathan's associates showed up to his store.

"Go to the back room and shut up! Don't say nothing, or you will die," he growled at me.

From the back room, I heard Nathan discussing a drug deal with the other man. After they finished the transaction and the other man left, Nathan came to the back room to get me.

"We're going back to Walnut Hills. I've got some business to handle," he said.

In the car, I listened to Nathan's part of a phone call and learned that the man he had been talking to in the store was a Cincinnati police officer.

Once I was back in Walnut Hills, still on the run, I told some people who I thought were my friends what had happened. One of the guys then told Nathan that I said he tried to rape me. I believe the guy who told Nathan was vengeful because I resisted his sexual advances.

Nathan sent a message to me, through some other people, "She had better keep her mouth shut before people find her body somewhere, stinking."

At another point when I was on the streets, my mama and her friend Eve came to look for me. Eve was driving, and they chased me through an alley. This alley was right behind Christ Emmanuel Christian Fellowship. When I reflected over this, I realized I was running from God. Then years later, God had me walking through that same alley to go and serve his people. At the time I was running away from my mama and her friend, I ran so fast that the baseball cap I was wearing flew right off my head.

Shortly after that incident, my Aunt Vesta sent word through one of my associates, Ramone, that she had some money for me—if I would come see her. People often talk, and both sides of my family were influential and respected.

Ramone was like, "I will take the money to her."

I knew that my aunt was not going to go for that, and she sent word for me to come to her. Unbeknownst to me, that was the setup to get me home. It worked.

Later my aunt told me that it had been my daddy's idea. He knew what would draw me in. The money. When I got home, my aunt had me go to the laundromat with her. She fed me, and I went to sleep while she was washing her clothes. Once my aunt's laundry was finished, we went back to her home, where I went back to sleep. I was exhausted from being on the run.

I was unaware that my aunt had called my grandmother, who is her mother. Grandma had called the police. To be honest, looking back, I was so glad that my grandma called the police because I was tired of running, but I needed something serious to make me stop.

I was booked at the juvenile detention center in Hamilton County. I was there for approximately two weeks. Those were the longest days of my life. My room was the size of a walk-in closet—certainly not what I was used to. I thought, *I wanted freedom. If this is the end result of my search for freedom, I had traveled the wrong path.*

I didn't even have the walk-in-closet-size cell to myself. I had a cellmate, and to make matters worse, she was suicidal, and she tried to hang herself while I was there. The staff moved me to a different cell because they had to strip my cellmate naked. She couldn't have anything with her that she could possibly use to harm herself.

My experience in Hamilton County 20/20 convinced me that was not the life I wanted for myself. I called my mama and begged, "Please get me out of here. I promise not to run away again."

But Mama was not having it. She made me stay there until my court date.

As you can imagine, I was angry, cussing and fussing, which did not change anything. As a matter of fact, it showed my mama that I wasn't ready to get out. I had not learned my lesson yet. Each day grew longer and longer. I intensely missed all of the comforts of home. I couldn't go to the refrigerator when I wanted to go. I did not have my comfortable bed or clean shower. I didn't even have my own space. I had come to the conclusion that incarceration was not for me.

On my last day there, I was at breakfast waiting to go to court.

"You better eat. It will be a long time before lunch," Ms. C. said. The corrections officer's outer appearance was attractive, yet the inner perspective of her mind was negative. If I did not have a strong personality, she would have broken me even further down than I already was.

"I'm not eating because my mama is getting me out of here," I responded.

Ms. C. smacked her lips and rolled her eyes at me. I did not care because I knew that I was leaving, and after court I did.

During my court hearing, the judge assigned temporary custody of me to my father's mother. I also had to go to counseling.

That might sound promising, but the truth of the matter was the therapist who the Hamilton County Court System assigned to me was whack. He was not helpful at all. He would not even look me in my eyes. He had nothing much to say. It was almost like he was a statue in the room. He was just like most of the people in my life: nonattentive and disinterested.

After one particularly useless session, my grandmother told him, "We aren't going to keep catching the bus from College Hill to Norwood for this. All Erica does is get on the phone with her friends and mock you."

After that visit, the therapist asked the courts to assist in finding me a new therapist.

My time with my paternal grandma was great! I did not feel like a prisoner. I caught the bus to school from her house. Grandma split my child support money with me. Everything was amazing! I could spend time together with my neighborhood friends and my favorite aunt, Aunt Vesta, and her children. Life was a breeze!

Who in your life made life a breeze?

_____

_____

_____

_____

_____

_____

_____

_____

_____

_____

How did time with that person shape you and your story?

_____

_____

_____

_____

_____

_____

_____

Looking back, what do you wish you could tell that person?

Erica Anderson

During the time I lived with my dad's mom, I met my first baby daddy—well, at least I've always *said* he was the daddy. One day, my Aunt Vesta, her children, and I had just come from the United Dairy Farmers convenience store when I saw a tall, brown sugar complexion guy! My hormones went all over the place!

I had gone from my prisonlike maternal grandparents, to so much terribleness when I was on the streets, to freedom to do what I wanted to do with my paternal grandmother, so my crazy young mind thought, *This is it! This is the life I've been waiting on!*" Little did I know I was headed for even more destruction. But this time, I didn't have to run away to find it. I had an all-access pass.

At ages twelve and thirteen, I thought that I was grown. I thought that I had all the answers, and for real now, nobody could tell me anything.

I set out to know more about that handsome man, Colson. I studied him every chance I got. I just had to have him, so I thought!

A year or so went by, and I learned that he was a mentally, emotionally, and physically abusive thief.

Have you had any "thieves" in your life—whether actual thieves or emotional or spiritual thieves?

_____

_____

_____

_____

_____

_____

_____

_____

How did you cope with them?

_____

_____

_____

_____

_____

_____

_____

_____

_____

How did they impact your story?

_____

_____

_____

_____

_____

_____

_____

_____

_____

_____

_____

While I was living with my paternal grandma, my mama and my daddy had visitation rights. Although I couldn't have cared less if I saw them not, my grandma made me go visit with my mama because she knew that eventually I would have to go back and live with her.

That was a bad idea.

One time, when I was around thirteen-and-a-half years old and I was spending the weekend with my mama, her boyfriend Arthur was there. Yet again my mama was drunk, so she was unable to properly parent me. In the early morning hours while I was still sleeping on my mama's couch, that bastard crawled on top of me.

At first, I thought that I was dreaming. Then I wished I was. But it wasn't a dream.

"Arthur," I said, forcefully. "This is *Erica.*"

Arthur looked me in my eyes and responded, "You are lucky because I was about to tear some shit up."

Even after Arthur got up off me, I could not go back to sleep. I lay on the couch and silently cried. I wanted to get out of my mama's house immediately, but I could not leave because it would look like I was running away again. I had been told by the courts that if I ran again, I would be placed in foster care. I did not want that.

Hours later after Arthur left that day, I told my mama what had happened. I don't recall her having much to say or do about the situation at all.

The next time Arthur came back to the house, all Mama did was slap him across the face.

I was pissed. "Is that all you are going to do to him?" I asked. "That's it?"

Looking back, I know that Mama was afraid of him. He was the guy who had split her head open with a baseball bat a few years earlier. But I knew who was *not* afraid: my daddy's mama and my mama's daddy. After I told them what had happened, they both sent word to the bum that they would put a bullet between his eyes if he ever touched me again.

"Please don't tell the courts, Grandma," I begged because I did not want to go to foster care. "I promise that I won't run away anymore. I promise I'll protect myself when I must go back with Mama."

My grandma respected my wishes, but by the time I transitioned to live back with my mama, I had a tremendous amount of resentment built up for her. I made a promise to myself: *I'm going to do what I want to do.* Already in my life, I had been exposed to so much awfulness that I just didn't care anymore. I was numb. And clearly neither of my parents cared either.

Have there been points in your life where you realized the people who were supposed to love and protect you didn't or times when you realized the people who did didn't have nearly that much obligation to?

_____

_____

_____

_____

_____

_____

_____

_____

_____

_____

_____

_____

_____

While I was growing up, my mama was a functioning alcoholic. She never missed a day of work, and I never wanted for anything materially. My mama worked as a state-tested nursing assistant for many years, and she always had a second job too.

My daddy was a functioning crackhead. For many years, he worked for the US Postal Service. At one point, they sent my dad to a treatment center to get help with his drug addiction. My dad was also a welder by trade, and he helped to build the Paul Brown Stadium in Cincinnati.

Honestly, my daddy was not all that active in my life. Many times throughout my life, he stood me up, leaving me waiting at the door of my grandparents' homes—both his parents and my mama's parents. We would have plans, but he would never even show up. He always had an excuse. To the outside world, I was the problem, and those people often made comments such as, "How dare Erica show her behind the way in which she is." "Net does everything for her. She went to a private school. She keeps nicely dressed. She does not want for anything." "The problem is: Erica is too spoiled."

People had no idea how badly I was suffering behind closed doors. I needed so much more than material things. I needed a hug. I needed to know that my parents believed I could make it. I needed to be shown and taught how to love myself the way that God had in mind.

By the time I was around fourteen years old, I was sick of it all—-full of anger and confusion. I knew that running away didn't do the trick because they would just come looking for me. But I had a plan. I thought, *I will really get everybody's attention now.* I stole some medication from my mama's daddy. I planned to take the pills and end it *all. I'm done. There's no reason for me to go on,* I thought.

Again, my mama was drunk and did not know anything. I took the pills, then laid down on the bathroom floor sick. I did not even pass out—though at times I wished I would.

The next morning, my mama woke up, came into the bathroom, saw me lying there, and began fussing at me. Before I realized what I was doing, I grabbed her and began beating her like she was some stranger on the street.

"I hate you!" I yelled. "I wish you were dead."

I remember beating Mama's head to the floor. I could cry just writing this because to be honest, I really didn't hate her. I just wished our relationship could have been different. And I was doing to her what I had seen done to her over the years. When my mama and I would have these physical altercations, she never fought me back. In hindsight, I wonder if she felt that she deserved what I was dishing out.

Unfortunately, that was not the last time that I would put my hands on her. Over the next few months, I grew increasingly angry, sometime uncontrollably so. At that time, the only thing that got me through was prayer. I prayed because I knew that I was wrong. I did not want to hurt my mama, nor did I want anyone else to hurt her. I believe I hurt her because of the level of anger and resentment I felt toward her for allowing me to be exposed to so much. After each time I hurt her, I felt a deep remorse. It took years, but I often prayed and asked God to deal with the pain in my heart, and I cried out to the Lord for deliverance.

Have there been times in your life when you were at your wit's end?

_____

_____

_____

_____

_____

_____

_____

Did you ever consider turning to prayer?

How did it help?

_____

_____

_____

_____

_____

_____

_____

_____

_____

_____

_____

_____

_____

_____

_____

_____

_____

_____

_____

_____

_____

When I was fourteen years old, still with Colson, I got pregnant for the first time.

I have always been in tune with my own body, and I knew that there was a change. Even at that young age, I was aware of myself. I asked one of my aunts to take me to the doctor and get a pregnancy test, which confirmed what I had known.

My mama was furious—especially at the fact that I had not gone to her first. She took me to see a doctor, who said, "Erica at this time, childbirth should not be your focus. You have so much living to do. You will have time for that later in life. You will be just fine."

I wish I could have taken that doctor's advice. But her words were not good enough for me. I wanted a baby, and I wanted *that* baby from the guy who I was with.

My mama tried to explain, "A baby will make a boy/man run away quicker because most times they don't want the responsibility."

I just would not take heed. I thought a baby would make him love me more. Boy was I wrong. I soon discovered that he was cheating on me. I would leave out of the back door of his house, and he would have a girl coming through the front door.

My young mind thought, *Negro, if you play, so can I, and I am going to play better.* Mama set up an appointment for me to have an abortion.

I was completely devastated. I spent hours and hours at our local library researching abortions. I was terrified that if I had one, I would never be able to have children. Looking back, I wish I had been researching something more conducive for my life.

The people at the abortion clinic told me that it was my choice, but I knew that I could not go through a pregnancy and raise my baby alone. So, I got the abortion.

I felt so horrible. I was a murderer.

After a while, I started hanging out with my childhood friend, Shae, whose brother Tommy was good friends with one of my cousins. He also knew my boyfriend as well. We were all cool with each other.

There was a mutual attraction between Tommy and me, and one evening he and I were chilling at my mama's house smoking weed. One thing led to another. I had sex with him one time, and one time only, and I got pregnant. I did not think much more about it, as I was still in a relationship with my boyfriend, Colson.

During my early pregnancy, Colson got locked up for a carjacking. He was out of jail during the later months of my pregnancy. I recall a time while I was pregnant, he spat on me. I felt so low—like trash. That was how he saw me, and to be honest, that was how I saw *myself.*

My life was not freedom at all; it was even more confining that imprisonment. It was imprisonment within my mind.

My first baby, Camisha, was born in November 1994—when Colson was incarcerated again. He was locked up so often that he seemed to live in prison. But looking back now and understanding things better, I know that Colson had been imprisoned in his mind. And often that is the most difficult prison to break free from.

By that time, I had been with Colson on and off for four years, but finally I moved on because this time he was locked up for some years. He was not worth waiting for. It was a difficult time, but the unfortunate truth is that in the Black community, teenage pregnancy is common—especially when the dynamics are similar to mine or worse.

When I gave birth to Camisha, my mother quit work to take care of her so that I could finish school. She did not even get on welfare. Even with all my mama's dysfunctions, she tried to give me the opportunity to succeed after giving birth to my baby. Unfortunately, I was too stubborn and ignorant to recognize that at the time.

By this time, I was in high school—more or less. Mainly less. Because I skipped school so much, the truancy officer threatened to press charges on my mama. She was not about to go to jail for my stupid behavior. Her words exactly were, "I have *my* diploma, you gone see."

My daddy said, "Let me know when your mama withdraws you from school so I can let child support know, so I don't have to keep paying."

His words were my ticket out of school. I quit shortly after.

Thankfully, I did not inherit my parents' lack of value for education concerning me. In *my* home with my children, education is necessary. I was determined that each of my children would graduate high school, and so far, the first six of my eight children have.

However, after I dropped out of high school, the plan was to obtain my GED. I started out strong, then I met another guy, Geffory. He had smooth, dark chocolate skin, with waves in his hair that would cause you to be seasick. I had to have him! I got him when Camisha was eight months old, and we were together for the next eight years.

When I was about sixteen years old, I got pregnant again.

"You need to have an abortion," my mama said. "I'm already taking care of one of your babies. I'm not about to take care of another."

At that time, I was working as a state-tested nursing assistant at a nursing home called the "Jewish Orthodox." One of the women who worked with me, Eartha, approached me about my pregnancy and possible abortion, saying very negative things. I knew she was not saying it to encourage me to be better; she was gossiping about me.

When I told my mama what Eartha had said, my mama came up to my job to set that big mouth straight. When my mama got there and asked for Eartha to come outside, Eartha hid in the closet of one of the resident's rooms. She never said anything else that got back to me or my mama. She did what most people do: The ones who have the most to say have the least interest in raising a hand to help with anything.

Have you ever been plagued by gossips?

_____

_____

_____

_____

_____

_____

_____

_____

_____

_____

_____

_____

_____

_____

_____

_____

_____

_____

_____

_____

_____

_____

Erica Anderson

How did you handle it?

_____

_____

_____

_____

_____

_____

_____

_____

_____

What do you remember from high school?

_____

_____

_____

_____

_____

_____

_____

_____

_____

_____

How did those events shape you?

_____
_____
_____
_____
_____
_____
_____
_____
_____
_____
_____
_____
_____
_____
_____
_____
_____
_____
_____
_____
_____
_____
_____
_____
_____
_____

As time progressed, my relationship with Geffory became more and more toxic. I was battling my demons, and he had his. For a while, my mama allowed him to come and live with us.

My granddad thought this was a disgrace. Looking back in hindsight, it was. I would never have allowed my own children to do that. This made me disrespect Mama even more.

That season of my life was very dark and lonely—even though I had my family and friends around me. I was a church attendee, but there was no real substance concerning my relationship with God during this time.

I recall hanging out with two of my homies at Groesbeck Park in College Hill. We were sitting in a car, drinking Saint Ides and smoking weed. I was so intoxicated that I fell out of the car and hit my head on a concrete parking spot stopper.

My friends thought that I was a goner. They rushed me to my mama's house. I was able to hand them my key, so they unlocked the door and carried me upstairs to our apartment. My mama was in the apartment passed out drunk, but when one of my friends yelled for her to help, she jumped up and yelled, "Throw her in the shower with all her clothes on and turn on the cold water!"

To this day, I still have that scar on my scalp. When I wear my hair cut short, I can place a finger in that area, it might be approximately two to three inches deep. God was with me for sure that day. I could have died. When I think back, I can say that God has watched over me and protected me, even from my own self-destructive ways.

One might think I would have learned my lesson, but time progressed and I continued to smoke weed—just about every day. I was so depressed that some days I did not even want to get out of bed.

I was very mean and hateful. I did not want to be this way. I really wanted to be nice, especially to my mama, but every time I wanted to be nice, she fell drunk. She disgusted me. I was upset that she put herself in situations that could possibly end her life. When my mama was sober, she was good. The problem was this was not often. She was running from something. I will speak about that in later chapters.

I could not trust that Mama would protect my baby. For goodness sakes, she had never protected me. I did not realize it at the time, but I was becoming the person that I hated the most.

Have you ever reached rock bottom? When and how did you feel?

_____

_____

_____

_____

_____

_____

_____

_____

_____

How did that experience change your life?

_____

_____

_____

_____

_____

_____

_____

_____

_____

_____

_____

How did the way you were raised influence the way that you parent?

_____

_____

_____

_____

_____

_____

_____

_____

_____

_____

_____

_____

_____

_____

_____

_____

_____

_____

_____

_____

_____

_____

Camisha and me

Chapter 3: The Folly of a Fool

*"Stay away from a fool, for you will not find knowledge on their lips.
The wisdom of the prudent is to give thought to their ways, but the folly
of fools is deception. Fools mock at making amends for sin, but goodwill is
found among the upright."*
—*Proverbs 14:7-9 (NIV)*

I turned eighteen in January 1997, and in March I got my first apartment on Debbie Lane right off Reading Road. It was close to my family and on the bus route. At that time, I just wanted my own space, but I didn't want to be too far away from what was familiar to me.

It was a one-bedroom apartment, market rent, in a decent neighborhood—at the time anyway. I moved in, and my mama moved in next door to me. I felt as though I had accomplished something on my own. I had reached a goal on my own terms. And no one could tell me anything.

But the move was almost derailed at the last minute. I was waiting for that year's income tax refund to furnish it, when I received unwelcome news from the IRS: Someone else had claimed me on their taxes, so my refund was not coming!

I was furious! I was eighteen, and no one else had the right to claim me. I knew that it was not my mama. Then the IRS informed me that it was my daddy. I turned him in to the IRS because he did not have the right to claim me. He was not supporting me in any way shape, form, or fashion. I got my money.

Previously when I was 16 years of age, I recall my daddy telling me to let him know when the withdrawal process was completed for me to drop out of high school so that he could let child support know that I was no longer in school. Looking back on that as an adult, that showed his lack of genuine love and attentiveness for me. He showed me his *real* self. He was selfish toward me—always a taker.

I was born on his sister's birthday, who was murdered. I recall my daddy telling me that he felt as if it was his fault that she was killed because he was on the phone with my mother, when he believed that his sister was calling for help. Maybe he regretted my existence because of that?

My daddy treated his other daughter much better, and he was there for every aspect of her life! I was his firstborn. Why wasn't he there for me? I needed him too.

My mama was really all that I had, and that was not much. Outside of her dressing me and sending me to a private school, she was not there emotionally, spiritually, or mentally. I missed out on so much in my childhood. I had to grow up fast because of all to which I was exposed.

To be transparent, as a young mother I failed too quite a bit myself. But with a lot of prayer and opening my heart and mind to the leading of the Lord, my parenting perspective changed. I did my best not to expose my children to the life that I had been exposed to.

One time while I was living on Debbie Lane shortly before I moved out of that apartment, I went next door to check on my mama. She was passed out drunk. Her apartment was filled with smoke. I tried to get her out of there, but she would not budge, and she even began to fight with me.

I ran out of her smoke-filled apartment to go call 911 from the pay phone around the corner from our apartments. (That was before everyone had a cellphone and there were still pay phones on every corner.) The line was busy, so I ran across the street to the fire house.

"Please go help my mama," I begged.

The firefighters raced to my mama's apartment tried to identify the source of the smoke. They resolved that piece of the puzzle, concerning the smoke: My mama had something cooking on the stove, and she fell asleep.

When the firefighters attempted to get my mama out of the apartment, she fought with them as well. It was as if she wanted to die.

As I had so often felt during my childhood, I felt so helpless. About two years flew by. My relationship with my mama was still rocky. But one night while I was at work and my mama and I were on the phone, I was able to apologize to her for how disrespectful I was. I believe that was God giving me the opportunity to make things right before He took my mama from me.

One day while I was visiting my Mama's dad, he looked me in my eyes and said, "Prepare yourself for what God is going to allow to happen between you and your mother." At the time, I didn't pay a whole lot of attention to his cryptic advice.

About a week later, on May 18, 2002, Geffory, our children, and I visited his friend and his friend's wife. As the wife prepared dinner and dessert for us, she shared her experience with me about losing her mother. She urged me to appreciate my mama— no matter what we had gone through. While we were there, my stomach was cramping extremely bad, and shortly after dinner, we all went home.

The first Spider-Man movie had just come out, and we were all lying on the living room floor watching the movie. I began wrapping myself in the covers like a cocoon. I just could not get comfortable. I must have fallen into a restless sleep because the next thing I knew, Geffory woke me up and said, "Let's go to bed."

Around 3 am, I was abruptly awakened out of my sleep again by the telephone ringing. I missed the call, so I looked at the caller ID, which read "UC Hospital." I looked out of the window and saw that my grandfather's car was gone.

"My mama is dead," I told Geffory.

"Why would you say that?" he asked.

I just felt it.

I checked my voicemail. First was a message from my grandmother, "We are at the hospital with your mama."

Erica Anderson

The next message was from my mama's brother. "Your mama is dead."

I completely lost it. I felt like my soul had left my body. My entire body felt numb. All I could do was scream and run. I didn't know where I wanted to run to. I could not keep still.

I ran outside, and my cousin and uncle pulled up at the same time. I fell to the ground, and my cousin consoled me.

My uncle said, "I don't know why you are crying. You treated her like shit."

"Why would you say that?" my cousin asked. "It was still her mother." My cousin drove me to the hospital, but by the time I got there, the hospital staff had already taken my mama's body to the morgue.

I was crushed. I was her only child. For a long time, I was upset with my family for not telling the hospital to wait to move her until I got there. They took away my closure.

From the experience of losing my mama, I learned a hard lesson: Allowing a day to pass with anger against someone is not the way to go. According to Scripture:

"Be angry [at sin—at immorality, at injustice, at ungodly behavior], yet do not sin; do not let your anger [cause you shame, nor allow it to] last until the sun goes down."

—Ephesians 4:26 (Bible Gateway)

That lesson impacted me for the remainder of my life. I honestly have not been the same since. Does this mean that I will allow people to treat me any kind of way and just continue to allow them to bring emotional, spiritual, and physical stress to me? Absolutely not! However, I can forgive them and move on. It took twenty years to forgive my mother as stated previously. I had to work through layers and layers of anger, confusion, self-esteem issues, and insecurities. I can honestly say that I am grateful that God decided to allow me to get through the tumultuous storms that I have encountered throughout my life. I am forever and eternally grateful that I am not the person that I was then. And each day that God has granted me, I am better than the day that I was before.

When I was a little girl, my mama tried to make God out to be a big boogie man to scare me into acting right. But something inside of me could not agree with that. I am so glad that I know the truth about God's love, grace, and mercy!

My mama was supposed to spend the night with me and my children for Mother's Day weekend, which was a week prior to me hearing the message from my granddad. God was preparing me, but I really was not listening.

Of course my mama had been drinking, and she was telling my cousin how to manage his baby. I did not want to hear her mouth, so I put her out. To be honest what she was saying was not wrong. She went next door to my grandparent's home.

For Mother's Day I called my mama, and she was still talking about the same thing as the day before. I hung up on my mama. She tried to call back, and I failed to answer her call. That was the last time that I ever spoke to my mama, on Mother's Day 2002.

My grandma told me that my mama had dropped some food off for me and my children a few days after Mother's Day. I called to tell her thank you, but she never received the message. To write this, I had to relive that moment. It is hard when you love a person, and they continue to hurt themselves.

Years later, I found a letter that my mama had written to her friend, and this one thing stood out to me: "I can't wait until Erica really sees what life all is about." At the time that I found this letter, I was facing some things in my life. I bet you, I SEE NOW!

My mama had a life insurance policy for $25,000. I was the beneficiary. My granddad paid for my mama's funeral services because there was a delay with the policy due to my mama's drinking. So the deal was that I would give him his money back once I received the money from the policy.

As you can imagine $25,000 wasn't a lot of money, however I had a jumpstart to make that money work for me. Even after I would have given granddad his money back, I would have still been in a good place. Well that did not turn out so well. There were many influencers with their hands out. People who never had anything good to say about my mama or me, but they felt entitled to put their bids in on the money as if they were the beneficiary. I even had one individual steal from me. The bank was even trying to get over on me. They were lying saying that the check had not cleared, until I called the insurance company and the bank together and the insurance company quoted the date and time that the check had cleared.

Once I was clear to withdraw money from the bank, I did not give granddad all his money back. I was tricked into having the check mailed to another family member's house because they said my granddad was trying to control me, and the money. Sadly, I am not even close to those individuals to this very day.

Even Jesus said in Matthew 10:36: "Your enemies will be right in your own household!" Even my own father after being released from the penitentiary for smoking crack, was not there when I needed him most after the death of my mama. He came and visited me for twenty minutes, and after he learned that I did not have any money for him from the insurance money that my mama left for me, the visit was cut short.

My Granddad forgave me, and he continued to stay by my side. I am so grateful that I was an adult when my mama passed away. If I was younger, I more than likely would have been put in the foster care system. All I really had was my granddad and my children.

Do you have any regrets concerning past situations?

_____

_____

_____

_____

_____

How have you coped?

_____

_____

_____

_____

_____

_____

Have you made the necessary changes so that you may walk
in healing?

_____

_____

_____

_____

_____

If not, are you willing to make a shift in your own life?

_____

_____

_____

_____

_____

_____

_____

_____

Erica Anderson

Some people say that this story is a reminder about forgiveness, hypocrisy, and love. It also highlights the idea that just because someone has the power to do something, it does not neces-
sarily mean it is the best choice.

What events do you remember from your young adulthood?

_____

_____

_____

_____

_____

_____

_____

How did those events affect you?

_____

_____

_____

_____

_____

_____

_____

Have you ever lost someone unexpectedly?

_____

_____

_____

_____

_____

_____

_____

_____

_____

How did you recover from that loss?

_____

_____

_____

_____

_____

_____

_____

_____

_____

Gregory and Serenity

Chapter 4: My Secret—Exposed

"But everything exposed by the light becomes visible, for everything that is illuminated becomes a light itself."
—Ephesians 5:13

I was still unaware that Colson was really my twin's father, although as my babies grew older, and more and more people noticed the resemblance between Colson and the twins, I began to have second thoughts. Even Geffory and his family started to have suspicions about the twins' paternity.

This presented a major problem. I wanted Geffory to be their father so badly that I began to convince myself he was, and then I began to believe my own lie. I so did not want Colson to be the father of my twins. I screwed up big time! I cannot stand Colson's guts. He was mentally, verbally, and physically abusive to me. I wondered, *Why did I sleep with him again?* And hoped, *This will all go away.*

I did not want to hurt Geffory and his family because they really did love my children. Geffory even got their names tattooed on him. *Man, this cannot be happening. I done messed up now,* is all I could think. Truth be told, my pride would not allow me to tell the truth.

I used to think that my actions only hurt me. Back at the time, I did not realize that my actions were also hurting other people. To be honest, at times my actions destroyed relationships.

As time went on, speculation about the twins not being Geffory's children died down—at least so I thought.

When I was twenty years old, I got pregnant again, but that time Geffory and I decided to abort the baby. We agreed that we did not need any more children.

A year or so later, I was pregnant yet again, but that time I was keeping my baby. Geffory was the father! Our son Eric looked just like his daddy, which brought about more questions about why the twins did not. Geffory begged me to tell him the truth, but I just could not bring myself to do it.

One day when I out was with Geffory's Aunt Freda, we ran into Colson's parents. Colson's mother blurted out, "Them children look just like my son!"

I could have died. *It's over now,* I thought. *Things are about to hit the ceiling.*

Freda and Geffory were tight, so I'm certain she told him. At that time, Geffory and I weren't living together, and our relationship was on and off. After that, Geffory and I began to drift apart, slowly but surely.

Early one morning in June 2002, my eldest three children were at daycare, and it was just me and my baby, Eric, at our apartment at 1941 Clarion Avenue. I had purchased a newspaper because I needed to find another job and a new place to live. While living in the house that I was renting, two of my four children contracted lead poisoning. I learned this at one of their yearly physicals. I always made sure that each of my children was caught up on their immunizations and dental appointments. That awful diagnosis was overwhelming on top of everything else that I was faced with.

Reading the newspaper, I saw an article for REMAX. Now deep down inside, I knew that I was not able to buy a home, but I thought, *Why not.* My thinking has always been, *If a thing is meant to be, I will have it, and if not, oh well.*

So I called the agent who was listed in the article, and we got the process started. I should have known that they were shady because of certain things that they allowed, but I was desperate to move, knowing my babies were being poisoned in our apartment. Buying a home would be a big accomplishment for me. On October 24, 2002, I signed the deed on my first home— at the age of twenty-three. 5209 Saguin Street. Home ownership was both a blessing and a curse. Well, the coin flipped really quickly. I had been a victim of predatory lending. Not long after I had purchased the house, this company was on the local news for many scams resulting in predatory lending.

It was a blessing to own my own home, but the curse was that it couldn't have come at a worse time. It happened when I was at my lowest, barely working, and grieving the passing of my mama. I was in such a deep depression that I wished I was dead. It was as if I was living in a nightmare, and I would have given anything to wake up. I thought that my life was worthless, and I did not have a purpose for living. I did not even consider myself worthy to mother my children. What was the point? I had exposed them to so much. I was better off dead. They would have been better off without me.

I was tired of me. But even as deep in despair as I was, something inside me would not allow me to lie down and die.

Even in that, God still showed Himself faithful. He came through yet again for my children and me. While we were living at that house, the truth came out concerning the twins. One day, Geffory came over and asked the question again about the twins being his children. I still could not bring myself right away to answer.

Then Geffory said, "I took the babies to get a DNA test when they were with me. The results came back. They are not mine."

I could have melted all over the floor like butter on a hot skillet. But it was time. I had to come clean. I knew all along in my heart that Colson was the daddy. I just did not want that to be the case.

After that, Geffory and I really had a time. Every chance he got, he would throw this up in my face. He was no saint, and there were nights that he would not even come home. Nevertheless, I brought this circumstance upon myself. I knew that it was time for me to move on. After eight years of being with Geffory, I was not going to stay in a relationship where I was continuously reminded of my shortcomings.

Have you ever stayed in a situation knowing that it was not the best for you?

_____

_____

_____

_____

_____

_____

_____

_____

_____

_____

_____

_____

_____

_____

_____

_____

_____

Have you ever settled to keep a person or persons in your life to be accepted?

_____

_____

_____

_____

_____

_____

_____

_____

_____

_____

How did you handle the rejection?

_____

_____

_____

_____

_____

_____

_____

_____

_____

_____

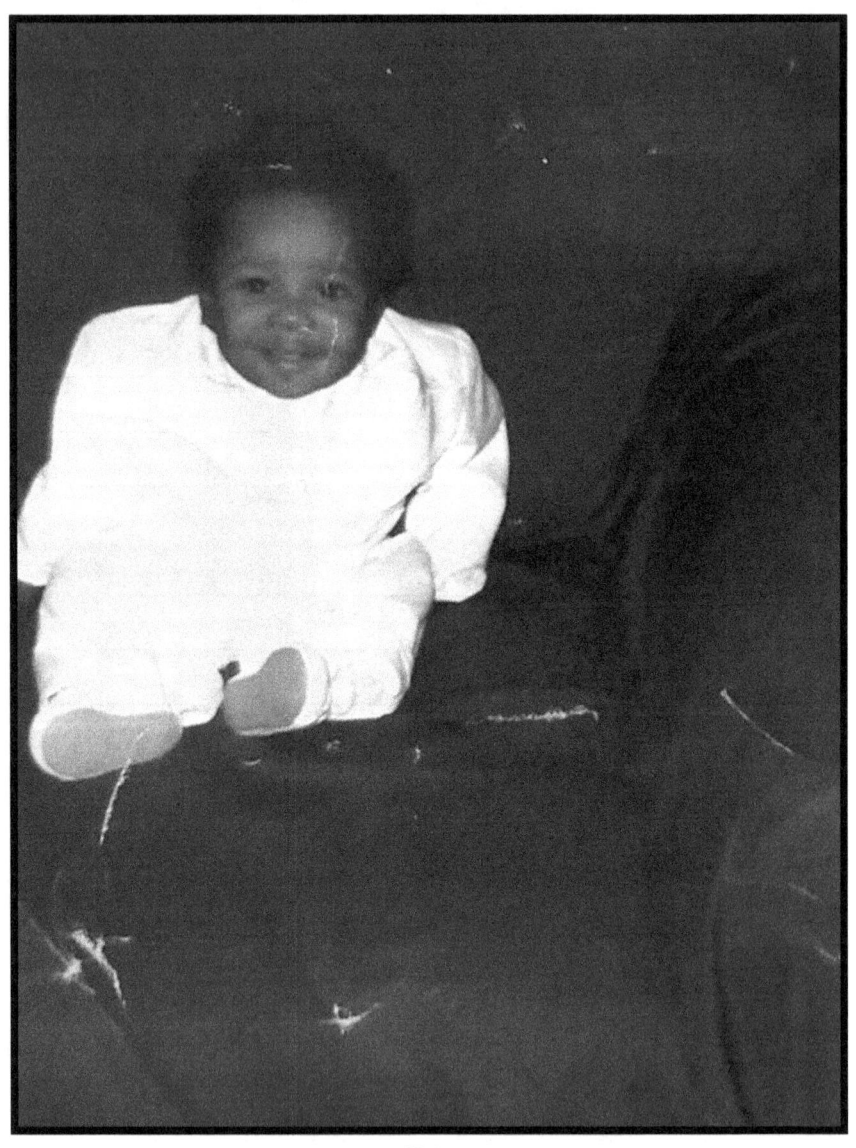

Eric

Chapter 5: Going Through the Motions

"And we know that in all things God works for the good of those who love him, who have been called according to his purpose."
—Romans 8:28 (NIV)

After my relationship with Geffory began to fall apart all the more, I studied and obtained my commercial driver's license. Prior to this I was working for a medical agency. I started out at First Student as a school bus driver, and I felt like First Student was playing games with me, due to the many delays of obtaining my commercial driver's license from them, so I got my class B commercial driver's license and got a job at Peterman bus company. I worked there for a brief time, but then I went back to First Student where I was employed off and on for four years. During my off time from First Student, I was gainfully employed by the city of Cincinnati Sanitation Division.

That's where I met my ex-husband, Dwayne, who I was married to for fifteen years. He was on light duty at the time, which means not out working on the trucks out on the road. Instead, he was tasked to take me and a few other new workers to get our uniforms and boots. When our eyes met, I was hooked.

An OG worker there picked up on my interest and said, "Baby girl, whatever you do, do not get caught up with these men here. They are a pack of wolves, and you are fresh meat."

I took no heed to the warning because I engaged in conversation with Dwayne, and sometimes those wolves approached me. I shut them down, especially because I had my eyes on Dwayne.

That day, after I got my uniform, I went home and told my grandma all about it! I even said, "God done sent me my husband!"

At the time, I did not even know his name, so Grandma said, "If you don't know his name, how do you know that he is your husband?"

"I just know it," I said.

Ironically, a few years before, one of my family members drew a picture of a man who looked very similar to Dwayne: same locs, eye color, and muscular build. I just about begged that family member to let me have the picture.

Before Dwayne came to my home for the first time, I told him, "I have a picture of you."

Dwayne looked at me weirdly, and to be quite honest I would have looked at me weirdly too. I would have stopped talking to me. But out of curiosity, he came over. Dwayne was speechless at first, after the shock, he agreed that the picture resembled him.

I will never forget the first day that Dwayne came to my home. We were sitting in the kitchen talking, and I was waiting on my daughter Camisha to be dropped off. I heard a knock at the door. "Who is it?" I asked.

"Geffory," came the reply through the door.

"What do you want? You need to leave. I have company," I said. I refused to let him in. We were over, the truth had come out, and I could move on. Eventually Camisha showed up, but it was a while before I opened the door because I thought that Geffory was still on my porch.

When I opened the door for my baby, I saw a huge card and teddy bear outside. I was sure that Dwayne was not going to talk to me anymore after that display. Over the next few months, Geffory made every attempt to stop Dwayne and me from progressing. In the beginning of my relationship with Dwayne, Geffory came to the house to pick up the children. Even though we were not together, he still stayed in my children's lives—at least for a little while. I know the truth was he did not want me, but he did not want me with anyone else. I'll never forget when he said, "You have four children. No one other than me wants you."

Later that day, Geffory and Dwayne ran into each other at Walmart. "Geffory gave me an earful about you," Dwayne later told me.

What Geffory did was sow a seed of distrust in Dwayne. Dwayne did not understand that when he listened, it influenced how he dealt with me for our fifteen-year marriage. One thing I won't ever do is listen to my new person's ex-person. You must discern the motivation behind the information.

Dwayne and I got engaged a year after we were together. He was going to surprise me with the ring, but we got into it. I had a gathering at my house with some family over and was smoking while they were there. Dwayne was upset by this, and he withheld his proposal to me. My dad had told me Dwayne's plans and informed me of how I had screwed up. The advice my dad gave me is so embarrassing coming from a father to a daughter, I cannot even disclose it. Leading up to our wedding, one of my cousins told me that my daddy and other family members were saying that Dwayne was not going to marry me because I had four children. What they didn't know was I was pregnant with my fifth child when we were six months into our relationship.

I gave birth to Arabia in August 2004, and my daddy and family had to eat their words on our wedding day, December 11, 2004.

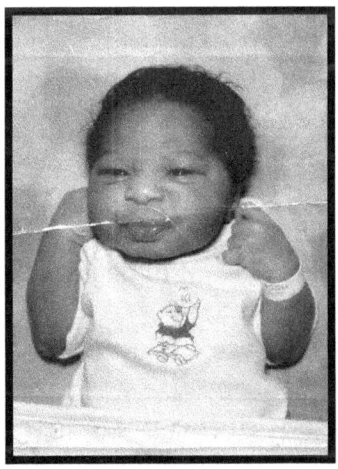

Arabia

Some people showed up to our small wedding just to see if it was going to happen. Honestly, I felt my pastor from my childhood church was glad that I was getting married because I now had five children out of wedlock.

At first, our marriage was amazing, but in time I experienced the old saying, "What comes around goes around." What I did not mention is that Dwayne was married when I met him. But I soon learned why it was so easy for his previous wife to leave him. His behavior was well described by:

For all that is in the world, the lust of the flesh, the lust of the eyes, and the pride of life, is not the father's, but is the world's.
—1 John 2:16

Without exposing certain details, yes God knew that Dwayne and I would marry, and God also knew that we were not going to last. We moved off fleshly desires—what I was used to at the time. Although over the years we did attempt to incorporate God into our marriage, plenty of other outside influences often reaped havoc in our household. There were many things that we could have both done differently. All the red flags were visible, but I wanted to do right and honor God, be a student of God's word, and be a wife, a mother, and serve my family and God's people.

Dwayne and I had two different life visions, and this destroyed any chances of us ever having any real substance in our marriage, especially because we did not have a solid foundation. Nevertheless, I was not about to give up on the one thing that I always desired: to be married. So even with the red flags of my ex-having an issue with women, I wanted to be a good wife. I figured that I had endured so much already from guys who were not my husband, why not hang in there with the one who I was married to. Plus, I did not want to be known as a failure by leaving my marriage.

Over time, our marriage got even more crazy, but by then I was pregnant with my son DJ. I was super excited to be pregnant with DJ because with this pregnancy, I was up under the marriage covenant. This was new! Finally, I could say that I was having a child the way God desired me to have one!

I was even rebaptized during that pregnancy, by both water and fire! To be baptized by fire is an example of receiving the Holy Spirit with the edification of speaking in tongues, and a host of other spiritual gifts. This was huge. As far as I was concerned, I was for sure on the right path.

In this season, I became judgmental and had forgotten that "Woe it is me." I thought that because I was on track, I had arrived. I forgot that ten or so months ago, I was in a jacked-up space. Years later, my sister TJ reminded me that I had become very judgmental.

DJ was born in April 2006—the sweetest baby, full of love and laughter! I always knew that the call of God on his life was great because of the circumstances of my pregnancy with him. Out of all my children, DJ has faced some of the greatest challenges. Nevertheless, he is still victorious!

When DJ started preschool, he would run out of the school. I believe that it was the teacher's approach. I would have been afraid of that teacher as well—she was scary and mean. Fortunately, I am not one who is afraid. I am one who will stand against injustice and systems that are hell-bent on destroying people. One thing that I have spoken against is the fact that there are two things that my Black sons have against them: They are Black, and they are males in America. Being the person I was created to be has allowed me to productively advocate on behalf of my children.

Are there circumstances in your life that you can admit you know did not have a solid start?

_____

_____

_____

_____

_____

_____

_____

Were you able to accept responsibilty for your actions that may have placed you in a not-so-favorable position?

_____

_____

_____

_____

_____

_____

_____

_____

_____

_____

Have you forgiven yourself?

Me holding DJ with Greg and Eric

Chapter 6: Separation Anxiety

A Psalm of David
The Lord is my shepherd;
I shall not want.
He makes me to lie down in green pastures;
He leads me beside the still waters.
He restores my soul;
He leads me in the paths of righteousness
For His name's sake.
Yea, though I walk through the valley of the shadow of death,
I will fear no evil;
For You are with me;
Your rod and Your staff, they comfort me.
You prepare a table before me in the presence of my enemies;
You anoint my head with oil;
My cup runs over.
Surely goodness and mercy shall follow me
All the days of my life;
And I will dwell in the house of the Lord
Forever.
—Psalm 23:1-6 (KJV)

Geffory was fighting me for joint custody of Eric, which put me under a lot of stress. I knew he wasn't fighting for joint custody because he wanted to do the right thing and be involved in his son's life. It was in retaliation for me breaking up with him.

I got sick, then developed bronchitis. I was exhausted—mentally and physically. One morning when it was very important for me to be up on time, I overslept. I missed my court appearance with Geffory to determine custody of Eric by about 20 minutes. Because I didn't appear on time, the magistrate granted custody to Eric's father.

It was almost like I had a premonition that something was going to happen. A few months before, I brought Eric into my closet with me and told him how much I loved him over and over. "No matter what people tell you, always know that I love you," I said.

Little did I know that a few months after Eric would be taken away from me. And Eric was *completely* taken away. Geffory wouldn't let me see him at all. The only time I could see him is when I visited him while he was at school. Because I had a rapport with the teachers and I was an active parent, the teachers allowed me into the classroom to sit with my baby while he was in school.

I sank into a deep depression and had my second nervous breakdown. It was a very dark time. My husband at the time, Dwayne, and my ex, Geffory, were embroiled in a testosterone competition, constantly telling me what to do. I wasn't about to bow down to anyone, but in the middle was my son, my other children, and me. My children weren't used to being split up like that.

Right after I left the courthouse that day, I hired an attorney. I paid him $500. Geffory hired another attorney for thousands of dollars.

When my lawyer stood to speak in court, I realized he had a stuttering problem. *I'm never going to get my baby back,* I thought.

But can you imagine, I did!

In February or March or so, I went to the hospital to have an early sonogram because I was pregnent again.

"I can't find what I'm looking for," the technician mumbled, then hurriedly left the room.

When she said that, I knew.

A doctor came back in with the tech, and he said, "We can't find the baby's heartbeat. We'll schedule you for a DNC tomorrow."

"Listen, doctor, let's not do this," I said. "Can we wait until Monday?" Somewhere in my mind, I was hoping that maybe they missed it, and my baby was going to be alive.

"We have to do it first thing Monday morning because poison could set up in your body," the doctor said. "You could die."

Dwayne and I named the baby Hope, and I went in Monday morning for the procedure. That sent me headlong into depression. I was bad off.

Dwayne didn't seem to miss a beat at the loss of the baby. To be honest with you, from him and Geffory battling and ignoring me, I felt like I was in this by myself.

The depression was heavy. I felt stuck. The only thing that helped me come out of that was my faith in God.

Eric came back home in March 2007. My baby had endured a traumatic experience while he was away from me. Him coming back home was hard. There was so much turmoil. To be honest, I could not wait for Eric to turn eighteen just so I would not have to communicate with his dad. We had shared parenting, and those first few years was hellacious. Even while having the shared parenting, his father was incarcerated for drug trafficking, but I knew that my son needed his father, and to be honest I was tired of fighting. I just did not have it in me.

A few months later, I was pregnant again. I thought, *It is what it is*. I was with my husband. I maybe wasn't thrilled to be pregnant, but I was going to love my baby, nonetheless. Fortunately, I found a community of people from our church who prayed for me, especially one elderly woman. I gravitated toward people who were older than me who had lived some life. They encouraged me to pull out of that dark space.

Another person who helped me through that hard time was my Aunt Rachel.

Although she's not my biological aunt, she's been more of an aunt to me than some of my own blood aunts have been. When I was feeling very low, she reminded me of times before when God had seen me through.

It was a good thing too because I was about to be handed another challenge.

Camisha, my oldest daughter, began running away from home. At various times she stayed with her family on her dad's side and my family on my mom's side, including my grandmother. One of my aunts, a cousin on my mama's side, and a cousin on my dad's side were all in on it. They were harboring her, encouraging her not to come home. That betrayal cut me to the core. God had another cousin who I don't even have a relationship with confirm this. Although she and I still don't communicate, I am forever grateful that she exposed the truth.

Camisha finally stopped running away after she gave birth to my first grandbaby. To this day, only the cousin on my dad's side apologized. The rest have not. I don't trust any of them.

Have you ever been betrayed by a loved one?

_____

_____

_____

_____

_____

_____

_____

_____

_____

_____

_____

_____

How did you cope with it?

_____

_____

_____

_____

_____

_____

_____

_____

Are you mentally prepared to forgive the people who have hurt you? Do you know the importance of forgiveness?

_____

_____

_____

_____

_____

_____

_____

_____

_____

_____

_____

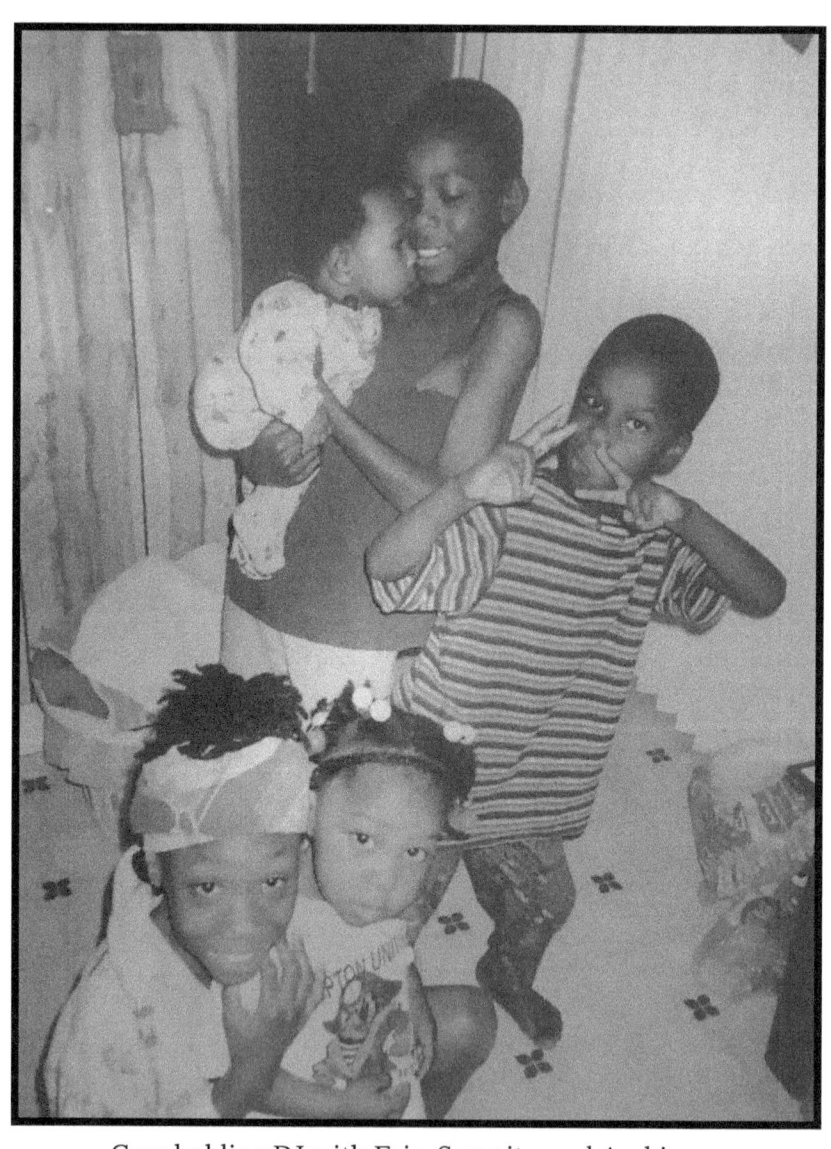

Greg holding DJ with Eric, Serenity, and Arabia

Chapter 7: They Counted Me Out, But God

"What shall we then say to these things? If God be for us, who can be against us?
He that spared not his own Son, but delivered him up for us all, how shall he not with him also freely give us all things?
Who shall lay anything to the charge of God's elect? It is God that justifies."
—*Romans 8:31-33 (King James Version)*

A few months after the miscarriage, I was pregnant again, with my son Amoz. I was 28 years old. During my pregnancy, I studied for my GED. I wanted to go to school to become a nurse. I didn't want to keep relying on these unreliable men in my life, yet I wanted more out of my life.

And the only way to get it is with an education.

So I was pregnant, caring for my other children, keeping house, working, AND studying for my GED.

Finally, test day came. I took the test, and while I felt good about it, I wasn't certain I had passed. While the family and I were out and about, my phone rang!

It was one of my teachers from Cincinnati State Technical and Community College. She had been supportive of me, honestly more supportive than my own blood—and a total stranger.

After I answered and recognized her voice, she said, "I called because I know how badly you wanted this: You passed!" I could hear the excitement in her voice.

I was so excited. It was so awesome. I received my GED in April 2008 after several attempts, and failure each time in the past, and Amoz was born in June 2008.

I was so happy to finally have my high school diploma after all those years. All school subjects came easy to me, except for math. That was a struggle.

With so much on my plate, thank goodness I was blessed with an easy baby. Amoz was a little sweetheart, an angel. I nursed him. I nursed five of my eight children.

Once Amoz could walk, he went right to running. He kept me running all the time. And to this day, he's good at sports.

I wanted badly to provide a better life—and a better future—for my children and me. I had been working as a state-tested nursing assistant. It was back-breaking work—literally. I remember one day taking care of one of my patients and my back was killing me. I had been doing that for sixteen long years, and I remember just taking a break, breathing, and thinking, *There's got to be more than this. This is not it.*

I thought becoming a nurse would be the ideal way to achieve it. So, in 2009, I started nursing school.

Unfortunately, I was not ready. I didn't take it seriously. I remember one of the first days of classes, the director came into our room, introduced herself, and said, "This is something to be taken seriously."

I didn't listen. I didn't study. Not that becoming a nurse wasn't valuable to me. It was. But I thought I could learn what I needed to learn in class and not put in the extra work and time studying at home. Clearly, I was wrong. So I didn't make it.

I went back to what I knew: Driving a bus.

And then I got pregnant again. I'll never forget how I found out. I was at the doctor's office with Amoz, who was not feeling the best. I recall thinking we both had a stomach bug.

"Wow! You're pregnant," said the doctor.

I thought, *Here we go again.* People would always ask me, "You pregnant again?" And I would say to them, "When's the last time I called to ask you for something for my children? Exactly." This most often caused people to label me to have a smart mouth. But the truth of the matter is people think that they can say and do you any kind of way and you are supposed to just keep silent. I wasn't having that, and I still ain't. It is called respect, it is reciprocal, if you give it you will get it. You don't have to like a person to respect them. Just consider how you want to be treated. And disrespect comes in all forms. So be mindful how you handle people.

Running after Amoz while being pregnant with Joshua was no easy task! And to make life just a little bit more interesting, at the same time I was pregnant with Joshua, Camisha was pregnant with my first grandchild who was born in September 2010.

One might have hoped that becoming a mother would mature Camisha. But no. She started running away *with* my granddaughter. Her family on her dad's side tried to trick her into signing her rights to my granddaughter to them. But it wasn't a legal document—just a note on a piece of paper. After Camisha got home with Tae'Mesha, her aunt called me to say, "You need to bring that baby back over here because Camisha signed her over to me."

"Let me tell you something," I said, steaming. "Camisha is a minor. Therefore, that little piece of paper that she signed for you is null and void. I'm the one running the show here, and Tae'Mesha isn't going nowhere."

They didn't know who they were playing with.

A tremendous blessing in our lives at that time was a lady named Kimberly, who ran the daycare all my children went to, Angels of Joy Learning Center. Kimberly brought my grandbaby all her beginning-of-life stuff: car seat, clothes, diapers, wipes, everything. She was an angel for me and my family in our time of need.

My son Joshua was born in December 2010. It was a natural birth—even though he was my biggest baby at almost eight pounds. By the time I had pushed Joshua out, I was exhausted, too tired to push out the placenta.

So I started hemorrhaging.

One of the nurses checked me, went a little white, and said to the other nurse, "I have to go get a doctor." I could tell it was an emergency by the panic on their faces.

The doctor rushed in, checked me, and said, "Erica, I need you to push now."

After Joshua was born, they had given me some strong pain medicine to help take the edge off the pain, so I couldn't feel correctly to push. "I can't push," I said.

"Well, if you can't push the placenta out, I got to go in and *peel* it off," the doctor said, clearly not looking like that was the better option.

"Well, you got to do what you got to do," I said.

So the doctor reached in there, and as he was peeling the placenta down to pull it out, I was backing up, crawling backward up the hospital bed. It was so painful, but I learned an important lesson. If the doctor hadn't removed that placenta, I could have bled to death. Oftentimes in life, God must pull certain things away from us so we won't bleed to death.

Joshua was the sweetest baby. Even as a little boy, he loved the Lord. He would run around the house praising God. Joshua was also very clingy to me. To this day, we are still very close.

Has God ever pulled something away from you to help you to heal?

_____

_____

_____

_____

_____

_____

_____

When did you realize that?

_____

_____

_____

_____

_____

_____

_____

_____

_____

How did it impact your life?

_____

_____

_____

_____

_____

_____

_____

_____

_____

_____

_____

Amoz, DJ, and Joshua

Chapter 8: Slipping Away

"Though my father and mother forsake me,
the Lord will receive me."
—Psalm 27

In 2011, I returned to nursing school at Cincinnati State/Great Oaks. This time, I was determined to succeed. This was the year that my grandfather left me. Granddad prepared me for the moment that he would not be here with me. His wise teachings made things easier for me when he was no longer here with me.

I remember one Wednesday afternoon in May 2012, I was taking Serenity and Greg, who were fourteen going into the ninth grade, to a jobsite for teens. The process to start the job was held at the Urban League. On our way there, I saw my daddy get off a bus on his way home from work. I wanted to drive him home.

"Come on, old man. Stick and move. I got somewhere to be," I said.

"I'm old. I can't go that fast," he said, then he jumped in the car.

"I'm going to take you home," I said.

A few days later, on Friday, I talked to my daddy briefly on the phone.

Then on Saturday, Dwayne, the kids, and I were shopping because Sunday was some family event.

My cellphone rang.

"We are at the hospital with your dad," my dad's sister said. "He had a massive heart attack."

I later learned that my daddy had been at his sister-in-law's house, cutting the grass for his brother, who was in the hospital. My daddy had a heart attack and collapsed in the yard. No one knows how long he laid there until some stranger saw him, walked up and knocked on the door, and told my aunt, "There's a man passed out in your yard."

My aunt ran out to try to do CPR to the best of her ability. Someone called 911.

My daddy was rushed to a nearby hospital. After the hospital stabilized my daddy as best as they could, he was air-cared to one of the major hospitals in Cincinnati, Ohio. Due to the circumstances of not knowing how long he had been with decreased oxygen to his brain, he was admitted to the Intensive Care Unit. He was in bad shape and put on a ventilator. That's where he stayed for the next two weeks.

On the evening of June 8, something told me to go spend the night with my daddy.

"I need to spend some time with my dad," I told Dwayne.

He understood, and I went to be by my daddy's side. I stayed up as long as I could, just watching him breathe, but I fell asleep around midnight.

Around 3 am, I suddenly woke up. I heard God's voice ask, "Do you trust me?"

"Yes, Lord. I trust you," I said. Then I fell back to sleep.

The next morning, I awoke around 8 am. I moved across the room and sat next to my daddy on his bed. I said, "I used to always want you to be there for me, but I'm here for you now." I wanted to say a whole lot more, but these are the only words I could get out.

Then I left, went home, and crawled into bed.

I was awakened by a phone call from my aunt, who said, "Erica, your father passed away."

I believe he died from a broken heart because the year before, one of his very close brothers had passed away.

The hospital tried to tell me my daddy pulled the plug on his equipment. I knew from my nursing training—not to mention good old fashioned common sense—that brain dead people don't pull out plugs. I know in my heart his wife told the hospital to pull his plug.

Nothing would have surprised me.

Now both of my parents was gone. But I'm going to tell you the Scripture God inspired me to go to in the Bible. When you have a relationship with the Lord and believe in Him by faith, you have access to the Holy Ghost, who will guide you when times are tough.

Psalm of David.
The LORD is my light and my salvation; whom shall I fear?
The LORD is the strength of my life; of whom shall I be afraid?
When the wicked, even mine enemies and my foes, came upon me to eat up my flesh,
They stumbled and fell.
Though an host should encamp against me, my heart shall not fear:
Though war should rise against me, in this will I be confident.
One thing have I desired of the LORD, that will I seek after;
That I may dwell in the house of the LORD all the days of my life,
To behold the beauty of the LORD, and to enquire in his temple.
For in the time of trouble he shall hide me in his pavilion:
In the secret of his tabernacle shall he hide me; he shall set me up upon a rock.
And now shall mine head be lifted up,
Above mine enemies round about me:
Therefore will I offer in his tabernacle sacrifices of joy;
I will sing, yea, I will sing praises unto the LORD.
Hear, O LORD, when I cry with my voice:
Have mercy also upon me, and answer me.
When thou saidst, Seek ye my face; my heart said unto thee,
Thy face, LORD, will I seek.
Hide not thy face far from me;

Put not thy servant away in anger:
Thou hast been my help;
Leave me not, neither forsake me, O God of my salvation.
When my father and my mother forsake me,
Then the LORD will take me up.
Teach me thy way, O LORD,
And lead me in a plain path, because of mine enemies.
Deliver me not over unto the will of mine enemies:
For false witnesses are risen up against me, and such as breathe out
cruelty.
I had fainted,
Unless I had believed to see the goodness of the LORD in the land of the
living.
Wait on the LORD:
Be of good courage, and he shall strengthen thine heart: wait, I say, on
the LORD. Pslam 27:1-14 (KJV)

My parents couldn't help dying. But God reassured me that no matter what, He would always be with me.

I learned one important thing: When God asked me did I trust Him on that early morning when I was with my daddy, it wasn't just for that moment. It was for the rest of my life.

Three days after my dad died, my oldest son, Greg, was running a fever and had a seizure. He was rushed to Cincinnati Children's Hospital, where he was put on a ventilator. It was almost too much to bear. Thank God, Greg recovered quickly.

Have you ever had a moment touched by God?

_____

_____

_____

_____

_____

How did it affect you?

_____

_____

_____

_____

_____

_____

_____

_____

Has a loss ever transformed your life?

_____

_____

_____

_____

_____

_____

_____

_____

Chapter 9: A Dream Realized

"For as the heavens are higher than the earth, so are my ways higher than your ways and my thoughts than your thoughts."
—*Isaiah 55:9 (ESV)*

After my daddy got sick and passed away and my son Greg got sick and healed, I tried to keep putting one foot in front of the other. In December 2012, I graduated from nursing school!

I was jubilant, having finally met a goal that I had for so long—against all odds. And I mean that literally: I found out that some of my teachers had a betting pool that I wouldn't graduate because I had eight children.

Yes, I have eight children, which didn't make it easy. But, I have eight children, and I learned a thing or two along the way! Also I developed a pound of perseverance and a ton of tenacity.

The graduation ceremony was really nice. My husband and children were there. (Well except Camisha, who had run away again.) One of my cousins on my dad's side came. Maybe one of my aunts. I can't remember.

After graduation, before I could get a job as a nurse, I needed to pass my nursing boards. I studied like crazy with a nurse testing coach, and I took the boards on April 19, 2013. I didn't have a reliable vehicle, so no easy way to get to Pearson Vue in Mason, Ohio, to take them. I asked my aunt on my mom's side if I could borrow hers. She said no. I couldn't think of anyone else to ask.

I hit a big, bad, brick wall. I wanted to quit, throw in the towel. Just then, the support I needed came from an unlikely place.

"Erica, you've come this far. You got to keep going," my husband Dwyane said.

And it helped me push through.

I decided to drive our van anyway, and we made it there safe and sound.

I sat down at the computer, focused with all my might, and took the test. When I got to 88 questions, the test shut off! I knew that could mean one of two things.

I had failed very badly.

Or I had aced it.

And I had no idea which I had done.

When our rickety old van got me home, I called my nurse testing coach. She told me a secret, "Erica, go to the nursing board and try to reregister for the test."

"Okay," I said, turning to my computer. "I can't reregister."

"Congratulations!" my coach exclaimed. "You passed the boards! You got your license!"

The lightbulb went on for me: Because I had passed, I didn't need to reregister. If I had failed, the system would have let me reregister.

At that time, I had been working as a state-tested nursing assistant at a nursing home in Cincinnati called Twin Towers, so I started working as a nurse there. That was hard because the aides could not be receptive to me because I was the aide, just like they were just not long before that. I stayed there for a while anyways, and then I found another little as needed job where I worked at. And then I got hired at TriHealth hospital on January 6, 2014.

I have always wanted to be a nurse, so achieving this goal, although all odds were stacked against me, gave me hope to know that I could achieve anything that I put my mind to. Especially with all the opposition that I had faced, with losing my daddy while in nursing school, having my oldest son in the hospital three days after my daddy died, and having my eldest daughter running away from home all at the same time. If I made it through all of that with one of the greatest tasks of my life, I could endure anything that comes my way. I will finish what I start! I am not a quitter!

"What then shall we say to these things? If God is for us, who can be against us?
—*Romans 8:31 (ESV)*

My marriage had been crumbling for a long time. Dwayne's issue always was women. I was his third wife. I was about to leave him, then we received some horrible news. Dwayne was diagnosed with a brain tumor.

Here I was a young wife. I had endured so much loss already and now this. Dwayne had to have major surgery. I would never kick a person when they are down. I felt like I was supposed to stay. Dwayne had his surgery on June 25, 2014. Dwayne had a stroke while in surgery.

The only solace that I had in this season of my life was the fact that I had God and the body of Christ. The body of Christ was my family. My own family said when Dwayne had his surgery that they would get my children a bucket of chicken, if they got that chicken my name isn't Erica. And my name is Erica. A group of women from the church got together and prepared meals for my children the entire time that I stayed at the hospital with my husband.

After staying in the hospital for two weeks, the insurance company was ready for him to go to a nursing home for further therapy. But I wasn't about to let that happen because nursing homes don't care for your loved ones like you will.

I told the doctor, "Because I am a nurse, I will take care of him at home and take him to outpatient therapy."

While Dwayne was off from work, our bills kept rolling in. I could only work minimally, and on top of that I had to continue to maintain my home for my children. One day while at the grocery store, Dwayne and I had an argument about bills. I lost my cool. I went into the store, afraid that I would not have enough money to get food. I ran into a woman of high degree within the body of Christ. She asked how we were holding up, and I just kept it real with her. She took me to the customer service counter and purchased a $500 Kroger gift card for our family!

Another member of the body of Christ took one of our sons school shopping. We had ran into this man on a humble as well. He spent several hundreds of dollars on my son! God continued to look out for my family! Dwayne was back at work on October 13, 2014. Isn't God good?

After a while, thing's got worse again with us, and I was miserable in my marriage. One Sunday at church, Bishop gave the announcement about a class starting for those who felt the call to become a Licensed Minister.

That Sunday. I was beside my self, I wrestled with this. I had been told in the past that I could preach the Gospel. This is years before Bishop had made the announcement, but in my mind there is no way that God would choose me to do such a thing after all that I had done. Why certainly I wasn't worthy to speak on God's goodness on this level. I prayed and I pondered over this. God confirmed something for me, and I said yes to the call.

I had to have three references. One reference was one of my sisters in the body of Christ. I prayed and asked God to show me the other two. God gave me both, one was a Jewish man, and the other was my supervisor who was an atheist. Just remember this: God can use anyone when He has a plan for your life.

Has there been anyone you wished to purge from your life?

_____

_____

_____

How did you do it? Or how will you do it?

_____

_____

_____

Did it make room for new, more suitable people to come into your life?

_____

_____

_____

_____

_____

_____

_____

Have you ever had someone who may have different values advocate on your behalf?

_____

_____

_____

_____

_____

Could you advocate for someone who may hold different views than your own?

_____

_____

_____

_____

_____

_____

Have you ever had to make a hard decision to preserve your own peace?

_____

_____

_____

_____

_____

_____

_____

_____

_____

Would you rather be comfortable and miserable, or uncomfortable for a short time, with joy and a peace of mind?

_____

_____

_____

_____

_____

_____

_____

_____

_____

_____

_____

Have you tried to uphold an image knowing that behind closed doors you and your situations are falling apart?

_____

_____

_____

_____

_____

_____

_____

_____

_____

_____

What changes are you willing to make for your betterment?

_____

_____

_____

_____

_____

_____

_____

_____

_____

_____

Chapter 10: An Ending

On June 28, 2015, along with several other men and women, I was ordained as a licensed minister at Christ Emmanuel Christian Fellowship. That day was different than any other day of my life. That was a different level. That was a great responsibility. I was shaking in my boots so bad. I wanted to just back out. I felt that I didn't deserve to do this. I thought, *What if I can't live up to the responsibility?* Maybe I had not heard God right. Maybe I was just imagining that I was supposed to do this.

When Bishop was speaking to the ministers in front of the congregation, I recall him encouraging us and reminding us how God/Jesus called and used those who were not qualified, and they were able to still get God's business completed, with the leading of the Holy Ghost.

I had to beg Dwayne to come support me that evening at the ordination service. He did not want to attend the service that day.

Looking back in hindsight, I realize I was more concerned about what other people would think if he was not there. I found myself often making excuses for him when he wouldn't come to church. What was later revealed to me is that Dwayne was jealous of this opportunity for me. God had him confirm just that. Per Dwayne, he wanted to preach. I remember telling him, "This is not what I wanted to do at all. This is what God Himself called me to do."

"Many are called, but few are chosen. Jesus is not laying out the doctrine of Unconditional Election but is saying that when God invites all to participate with Him in His rule and reign on earth, He does so without partiality or favoritism."
—Matthew 22:14

Erica Anderson

I recall one of the members greeting me one Sunday, "Good morning Minister Erica."

I responded to her, "Good morning, but you can just call me Erica."

She said, "I just want to show you some respect."

I said, "I appreciate that, but just know I will fail you. Please don't place me on a higher pedestal than necessary. I know that I am a minister, but just call me Erica."

It was still new to me, and I was still afraid of my own failure because truly I did not feel worthy.

As time progressed, I got deeper into my studying the word of God. I continued to have challenges, but now I could face them with more courage and strength than I had in the past.

Things from my past began to creep in because Satan was throwing everything at me. I stayed the course. I continued to press. My marriage began to fail even more, and my children were going haywire. In 2016, I learned some damaging news from one of my children about my then-husband. It time for me to leave him. She was eighteen when she told me and on her own, but I still had my younger children. I had to have a plan. I could not just up and leave at the time.

Where would we go? How can I give up his medical insurance? I wondered.

I stayed a while longer, but I had so much resentment in my heart for Dwayne. I felt trapped, and I had to seek therapy. It was a struggle just to keep my sanity.

On December 2, 2018, I baptized my son Joshua. I was the first woman to ever baptize anyone at Christ Emmanuel. What a blessing it was for me to be able to experience that with my baby boy! I was so nervous.

On December 21, 2018, we had a beautiful mime concert at the church, where God had allowed me to be the mime minister. Once again, God had shown up that evening. He was all in that place. I remember one of the songs that we ministered to is called "Cycles" by Jonathan McReynolds. That powerful song spoke to my circumstances at the time.

After that, it all went down. The attacks intensified. My marriage was pretty much over. I knew that I was leaving Dwayne. And I did in 2019, after fifteen years of marriage. I did not have anything left. I was there physically, but I had left emotionally, spiritually, and mentally in 2014 prior to his brain surgery.

My children and I moved into a spacious three-bedroom home in College Hill. I left with nothing, but God blessed me in abundance.

When the Covid-19 pandemic hit, I lived in overflow, and I did not know that it was going to set me up to be able to relocate for good! I was in a new, complicated relationship that had many ups and downs. I learned so much about myself at the time. And to be honest, I can say the impact that man had on my life prepared me for where I am currently. We were in a relationship for three years, and he made me know that I will not settle just to have a man in my life, nor will I sell myself short. He made me know that I am valued by God, although during that dark season in my life, I had walked away from God because I knew that I was not living the way that I should have been. And I did not want to play with God. I don't need a title to make me feel good about myself. What God sees and knows about my secret moments is far more important to me.

Truth be told, although I had walked away from God, it did not excuse my disobedience to him, for not fulfilling the assignment on my life. And to top it off that man did not believe in God. If I can be honest at this season in my life, I thought that I needed this man so much until I was willing to walk away from God.

Even my children saw the change. They devised a plan to get him out of my life for good, and it worked. I wish him the absolute best because as I recall Romans 8:28: *And we know that God works all things together for the good of those who love Him, who are called according to His purpose.*

I am also reminded of John 10:29 (KJV): *My Father, which gave them me, is greater than all, and no man is able to pluck them out of my Father's hand.*

One thing about God is there is nothing in our lives that takes Him by surprise, so He has already made a way of escape, from all your troubles when you believe in His son, Jesus! I have not lost my mind because of my relationship with the Lord. Not a religious encounter, but this love relationship with the Father through His son, Jesus Christ!

For by grace are ye saved through faith; and that not of yourselves: it is the gift of God:
Not of works, lest any man should boast.
—Ephesians 2:8-9 (KJV)

Who and what are you willing to lose to follow Christ?

_____

_____

_____

_____

_____

_____

_____

_____

_____

_____

_____

_____

Have you found yourself desiring more tangible things and still feeling empty?

_____

_____

_____

_____

_____

_____

_____

_____

What is your life worth to you?

_____

_____

_____

_____

_____

_____

_____

_____

_____

Erica Anderson

When have you needed to summon courage?

How did you do it?

_____

_____

_____

_____

_____

_____

_____

_____

_____

_____

_____

_____

_____

_____

_____

_____

_____

_____

_____

_____

_____

_____

_____

_____

Chapter 11: A New Beginning

"See, I am doing a new thing! Now it springs up; do you not perceive it? I am making a way in the wilderness and streams in the wasteland."
—Isaiah 43:19 (NIV)

Shift = is often associated with change, growth, and transformation. It represents God's plans for our lives and can be challenging, but through faith and obedience, we can embrace it and experience blessings and purpose.

I was troubled on every side, literally! My children, finances, family, the law, and relationship. Everything that could go bad was happening all at once. It was the start of me recognizing that I was having anxiety attacks, and my blood pressure was high. All the pressure of life hit me at once. Yes, I had endured more than my fair share over the years, but at least then there were some breaks in between.

Not in this season! The Covid-19 pandemic was not the issue for me. It was people. I had come to realize that I was no longer going to live in the shadows of folks. I was at a breaking point. For real, I was tired of being tired. People did not value or respect me because they saw I had a lack of self-worth.

I was in a spiritual battle. I needed to break free from the prison of just enough, the prison of drama, the prison of explaining myself to people who did not care anyway, the prison of staying silent when I needed to be speaking, and the prison of speaking when I needed to be silent.

I cried out to God, and from a broken place I asked Him what was next. God confirmed for me every step of the way. Every single detail, God laid it out before me. God provided the finances. During Covid, I was furloughed from the hospital, and unbeknownst to me God was saving money in my retirement account, which provided more than enough money for me to go to an unknown place that He (God) was sending me to, Greensboro, North Carolina. I did not know anyone here. I was simply obeying the call of God on my life. To be honest, I had never even heard of Greensboro.

As a little girl, I used to imagine myself going somewhere far away from all of my troubles, now here I was 40 years later far away from my starting point with a different mindset. I allowed my dreams to become real in my life.

Even then when I was a child, God had a vision, deep down on the inside of me, that was far beyond anything I had ever known. Oh, trust and believe I had plenty of opposition getting here. While I was packing, I found a letter from a friend, who was incarcerated, who wrote, "Whatever you do, do not ever allow anyone to sit on your wings." Who knew years later that I would need to be reminded of this message.

You see, the worse prison is the prison of the mind. He nor I knew that his words would impact my life in such a positive, major way. Based on 1 Corithians 1:27 from the amplified Bible: *But God has selected [for His purpose] the foolish things of the world to shame the wise [revealing their ignorance], and God has selected [for His purpose] the weak things of the world to shame the things which are strong [revealing their frailty].*

After I got here to North Carolina, in my flesh and moving off emotions I ran right back to Egypt (Cincinnati, Ohio). I paid for my disobedience. At one point, I had a head-on car collision, and I was homeless, sleeping in my car for acknowledging that I knew God was still going to come through for me and mines. Thankfully, God did not hold my disobedience against me. God provided. He allowed me to sustain my place in North Carolina and a place in Cincinnati, Ohio, at the same time. And God blessed my babygirl to graduate in Cincinnati, Ohio, from Gamble

Montessori, valedictorian with a full ride scholarship to "Thee Ohio State University." She wanted to finish up at her school, and God provided.

Some would ask why did I not wait until she graduated. Well, guess what, my steps are ordered by the Lord, and we did not miss a beat. Have there been challenges? Yes. However, I believed to see the goodness of the Lord in the land of the living and now I am reaping the benefits! I know God's voice, and NOT another will I follow. My yes to God set me up for the rest of my days.

I am here to tell you from firsthand experience that if you want to know which direction to take in your life, seek God through His word, the Bible, and prayer. He will never lead you astray. Pray for and about everything!

I never saw these blessings coming, I am sure glad that I listened to the Lord. I am not trying to force what I believe on anyone. I just know what has been working for me, and I have no regrets, not even the hard times, because they have shaped me, and I have endurance and hope as a result! This is one of my favorite scriptures.

"Trust in the Lord with all your heart
and lean not on your own understanding;
in all your ways submit to him,
and he will make your paths straight."
—Proverbs 3:5-6 (NIV)

If you desire to have a relationship with God through His son, Jesus Christ, knowing that when the troubles of life show up, you will be able to endure with patience and you will be victorious in the outcome. I invite you to say with me.

Have mercy on me, O God, because of your unfailing love. Because of your great compassion, blot out the stain of my sins. Wash me clean from my guilt. Purify me from my sin. For I recognize my rebellion; it haunts me day and night. Against you, and you alone, have I sinned; I have done what is evil in your sight... Purify me from my sins, and I will be clean; wash me, and I will be whiter than snow. Oh, give me back my joy again; you have broken me—now let me rejoice. Don't keep looking at my sins. Remove the stain of my guilt. Create in me a

Erica Anderson

clean heart, O God. Renew a loyal spirit within me. Do not banish me from your presence, and don't take your Holy Spirit from me. Restore to me the joy of your salvation, and make me willing to obey you... The sacrifice you desire is a broken spirit. You will not reject a broken and repentant heart, O God.

—*Psalm 51:1-17*

God has the power to bring about a shift in circumstances that seem impossible or stagnant. This verse highlights the fact that God is always working in the world, bringing about new growth and transformation even during barren or difficult situations. He can create a way where there seems to be no way, providing streams of life during the desert.
Are you ready for the shift in your life?

What changes would you like to see implemented?

_____

_____

_____

_____

_____

_____

_____

_____

_____

_____

_____

_____

_____

_____

_____

_____

_____

_____

_____

_____

_____

_____

Letters and Prayers to My Children and Parents

Camisha

In November 1994, I gave birth to one of the most beautiful chocolate doll babies I had ever laid eyes on. Camisha smelled so good, and she had a head full of curly black hair and mahogany brown eyes that would cause a person's heart to melt.

Giving birth to Camisha was hard on my fifteen-year-old body. The experience was traumatic for me at such an immature age. I could sense the doctor's urgency, and that made me very afraid. I did not know anything about childbirth—until I gave birth to my child. It was terrifying. And the birth itself was hard because her head was a nice size. From the birth, I was split from front to back, and I needed to have at least thirty-six stitches. I lost so much blood. Later, my doctor told me that I could have died.

But God, seeing and holding Camisha made the pain and agony worth it.

Once I was able to get up and out of my hospital bed, I raised Camisha's little body up to God and dedicated her life back to God. I prayed, "Lord I give this child back to you. Protect and guide her throughout her life and allow her to love your first. In Jesus' name. Amen."

I did the same thing with my other seven babies, too. Even as a young mother, I knew I had to include God in the lives of my children. I needed Him to protect me and them. He has not failed us yet, and I do not believe that He ever will!

From before Camisha was even born, I knew that she was mine to love. I finally had someone to love me and someone who I could love back.

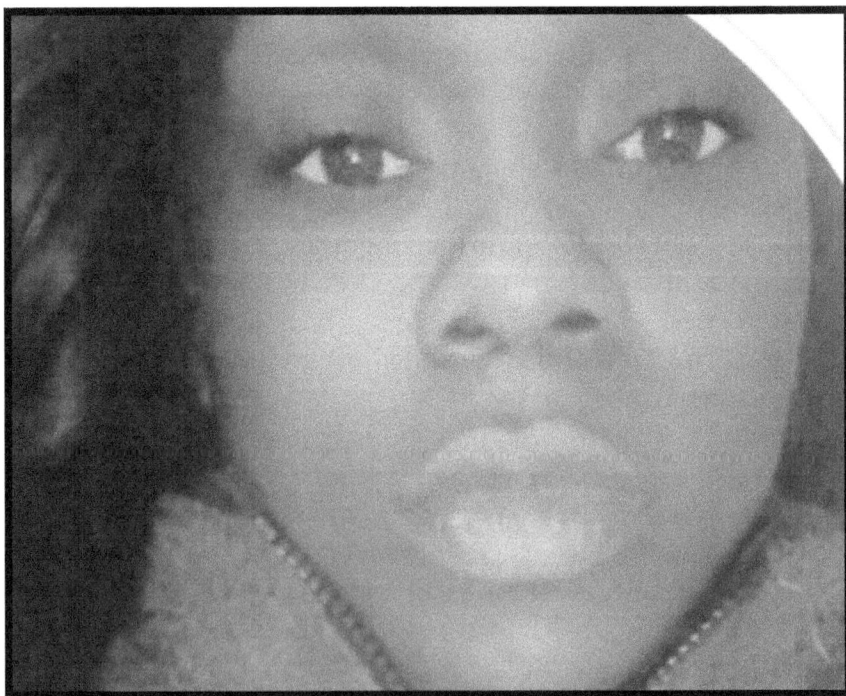

But I was fifteen years old, still a baby myself. I was not even in a state of mind to be able to give this precious gift what she deserved. I was so broken, so angry.

Even then, I knew that I wanted to keep Camisha safe from all the things that I experienced and endured. Years later, I learned that I did not do such a respectable job at that. I trusted people who did not deserve my trust, and their actions caused my first-born daughter resentment and pain.

Just writing these words allowed me to accept my role in some of her resentment and pain. And yes, I mean "writing" quite literally. I handwrote my book, then typed what I had written. I found the actual writing words on the page to be very cathartic.

My prayer is that my first love can find peace and forgiveness in her heart for me. Although we are remarkably close, our relationship is a rollercoaster full of twists and turns. I was there for all the major events in my baby's life, and I am grateful! There is so much more to our relationship, and I know that one day, she will tell things from her perception and perspective.

Camisha has blessed me with five wonderful grandchildren, and she too is making wonderful strides for her babies!

My Prayer for Camisha

Lord God, I pray that you bless Camisha from the crown of her head to the soles of her feet. Guard her heart and mind, oh God. Give her the strength to go on even when all odds are stacked against her. Give her the strategy and allow her to be open to the move of God in her life!

Lord, I pray for Camisha to be the mother that you have called her to be and protect and provide for her and my grandbabies.

In Jesus' name, Lord, allow faith to arise. Cause Camisha's desires to align with Your will for her life. In everything that she does, allow her to be victorious in Jesus' mighty name. Amen.

Dear Camisha,

You are the reason that I know how to love. You are the first of my bunch! I was ridiculed, called a "young whore," and thought to be less than, especially because my mama was an alcoholic, and my daddy was on crack. I was automatically written off, and because you are my seed, some people attempted to write you off, too, even to the point of telling you, "Ya mama was a hoe; therefore, you are bound to be a hoe."

But I decree in the name of Jesus that the devil is a liar. Yes, we have had our experiences, but remember, baby, our past does not dictate our future. I want you to be able to thank God even at your lowest moments. It is easy to thank Him when things are going your way, so do not get tricked. Develop a relationship with God that is not contingent upon your circumstances. If you stay focused, you will not lose as long as you put Him first.

I believe in you. I remember when you were ten years old, right before you started running away, you said to me, "People would run in the other direction if they knew the things that they were going to face." I never knew that even in that conversation God was preparing us for what we were about to face. I always had trust issues, or rather I just discerned the individuals who were full of crap. I am grateful that you are still here, despite all the people who thought that they were doing something by harboring you when you ran away! I have forgiven them; however, I doubt if I will ever trust them again.

Camisha, your name is a symbol of resilience and determination, reminding us that true strength is not just physical, but also emotional and mental. Your name carries a legacy of grace and inspires people who bear it to embrace their own unique beauty. It serves as a constant reminder that true elegance lies not in external appearances, but in the way one carries themselves with poise and dignity.

Always be yourself and do not attempt to fit in with the masses. Remember Matthew 22:14: For many were called, but few were chosen.

I love you always!
Sincerely,
Mama

The Twins

My twins' pregnancy was challenging. Because I was measuring large for my pregnancy date, at first, my doctor believed that I was further along in my pregnancy than we thought. But something told me early on that I was carrying twins! The sonogram proved what I already knew.

When my twins were born in February 1996, my little body was challenged! Serenity was easy going, and she did not hurt me when I was giving birth to her! She lived up to her name as such a serene little angel!

On the other hand, her twin, Greg, due to his stubbornness, came out twenty-one minutes later with a message to the world: Kiss my behind! He was born butt and feet first. He stepped into this world with that message, and to this day, he will not allow anyone to dictate anything to him. He stands on the promises of God concerning his destiny! God has promised me victory for my son and that no weapon that is formed against him shall prosper and that He would condemn every tongue that raises against him in judgment.

Although when my twins were born, Serenity was more laid back, today, she will tell you what is on her mind, and Greg is the more laid back of the two! However, neither of the two are pushovers!

When it was time for Greg and me to go home from the hospital, Serenity had to stay at the hospital because her suck reflex was not where the hospital staff expected it to be. Therefore, she had to stay in the hospital to ensure that she was able to eat on her own to be released. One of my aunts, also a mom of twins, advocated for us to get the hospital to release Serenity.

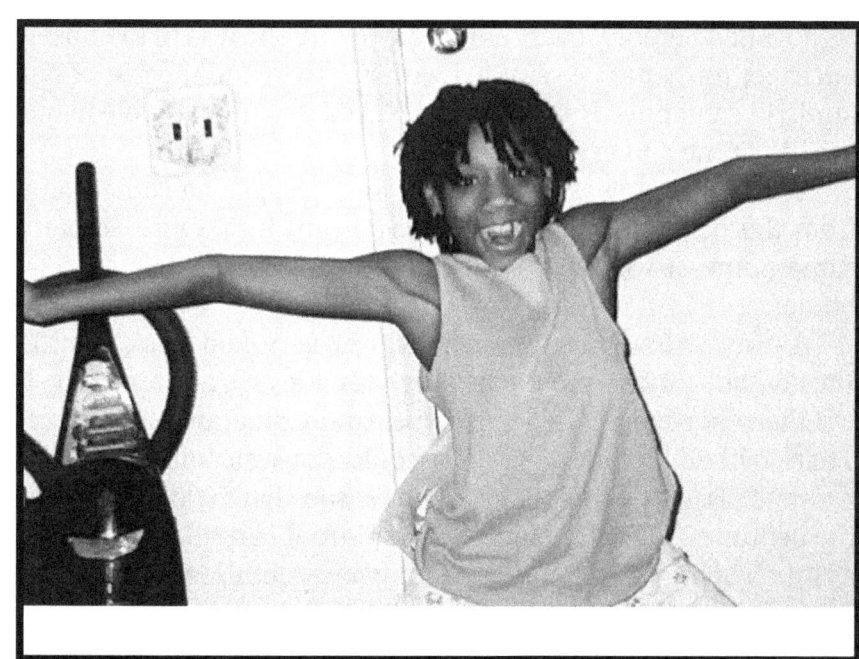

I visited Serenity every single day while she was in the hospital, eager for her to be reunited with her twin and the rest of our family! I can honestly say that this played a significant role in our bonding time and experience.

Because Greg was my first son and because he came home from the hospital first, I gravitated toward him. Once Serenity came home, it was such a blessing for both of my babies to be home!

As my twins grew, Serenity stayed very laid back, a little sneaky, but for the most part, she was a jewel, a serene angel! On the other hand, Greg was hyper and exuberantly energetic! That boy had so much energy, I could not wait until it was his bedtime! Truth be told, Greg is the reason that 2000 (8 pm) was the bedtime set in place for all my children! Parenting Greg took as much energy as parenting about twenty children.

Sometimes family members would label Greg as "bad." That made me angry to no end. I would say, "He is not bad. He is being challenged by the devil."

When Greg misbehaved and needed reprimanding, it seemed like he got more strength and energy. My family and even some of his teachers predicted that he would be a deadbeat—either in jail or dead. Ha!! Greg proved them all wrong! He graduated from high school right on time—with his twin.

Deep down inside, I have always known that I loved both of my twins, there has always been a disconnect between Serenity and me. To this day, I really do not know why that is. There have been many years of animosity in our relationship, due to my lack of empathy for Serenity's feelings. There was a time where Serenity reminded me so much of my mama and because of the unforgiveness that I had for my mother, I could not show empathy for Serenity for many years. I have since forgiven my mama, which allowed me to view my child in a different light and see where I failed Serenity.

As a parent, if there is any animosity between you and your child or children, I suggest searching deep within to get to the root cause. As parents, we are the first examples of how love

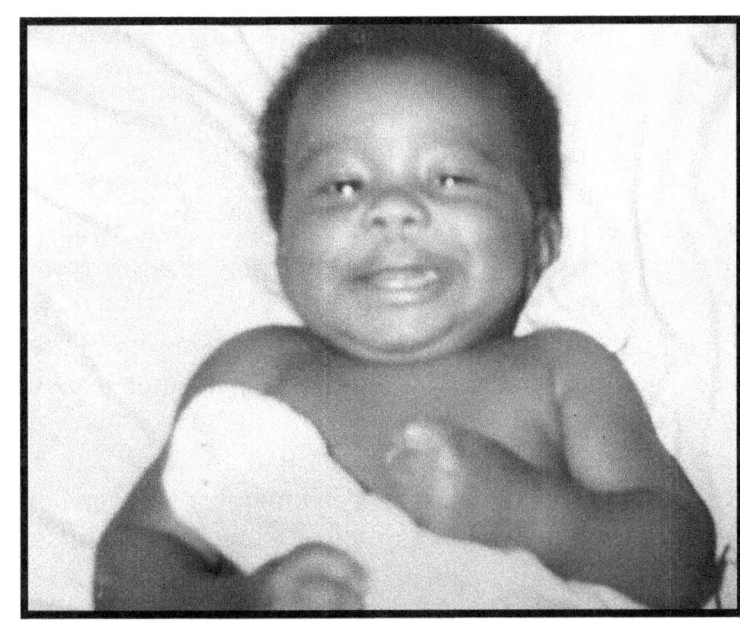

looks! We are the first to show our children how to have self-respect and to know their value and worth.

God intends an incredibly special relationship between a mother and her daughter, and I pray that God restores that relationship to Serenity and me.

I desire true healing for both of us in our relationship. I hope someday we can spend quality time together. I desire for Serenity to know that she is loved and valued!

To be honest, as a young mother with Serenity and Greg, I was very ignorant and unlearned. I really did not have an example of what a good mother was, with the exception of one of my aunts! She was married, and she had children. She prayed with us, and she showed her children and me love, even her husband's nieces and nephews she showed them love. Although as I got older I felt as though she and other family member's blamed me for decisions and choices that her children made that were not the best, although they had a mind of their own.

She was my only real example of motherhood, until I gave birth to my other four children by my husband. That is when I became a mother—not just a baby mama. I was involved in my children's relationship with the Lord, education endeavors, medical necessities, and troubles. I had been involved with these things prior to the other four children who I gave birth to. I stood up for my children.

Some of my children think that Greg was my favorite. Perhaps I favored him a bit as my firstborn son. Yet, I know that I have failed and disappointed Greg, and he has some fears because of that.

I have learned that children want to be heard. Allowing them to respectfully voice their perception of how things were will bring healing and freedom. Listen to them. Don't make excuses. However, state the facts, even the facts that lead you to be a screwup. Your children will gain more respect and compassion for you—especially if you genuinely did your best by them, although you might have had flaws.

Today, Greg is an amazing father and a husband-to-be! Both he and his Serenity are gainfully employed, strong individuals!

My Prayer for Serenity

Father God, I pray that you bless Serenity. I pray for the restoration of your relationship with Serenity. I pray that she will desire you with her entire heart.

Father God, I come against a spirit of confusion, and I thank you in advance for Serenity's victory over every obstacle that has been set before her as a trap to ensnare her soul. I thank you, Oh God, for deliverance from every evil thing in Serenity's life that is not like you.

Lord, I pray for Serenity's mental health. In Jesus' name, Oh God, please protect her mind. Give her peace regarding the word that you have spoken over her life before the foundations of the world. In Jesus' name.

I come against the identity crisis in Serenity's life. This is my opinion, and every individual has a right to choose how they want to live. However as for my children, the one who gave birth to them, although there were times that I have failed as a parent, I want them to have the absolute best concerning Gods word! Yes there are many times that I messed up, and as a young mother that is definitely expected. However, I have and am making the attempts to correct my wrongs, taking responsibility for how I failed. Though I know time will bring healing, I continue to encourage Serenity and her sibling in the hope and promises of the Lord concerning each of their lives.

I thank you for redirection and comfort for Serenity in you. I thank you for the wife and mother that she will be. In Jesus' mighty name. Amen.

Dear Serenity,

Baby, I begin by saying that I apologize for not giving you the attention that you deserved and required. I make no excuses. I was a young mother. However, I know now that I did not gravitate emotionally to you as a mother should have.

You were so soft and such a little angel, with your curly, coal-black hair and slanted eyes. Such a joy to have and to hold!

As a little girl, you never caused me any trouble. You were easy-going, and you loved your twin brother! Still to this day, you guard over him. You are feisty, sometimes without a filter, nevertheless, I can depend on you to be genuine and authentic. No one can ever accuse you of being phony. What they see is what they get.

I know that there is a huge side of you that carries out love and justice. Serenity, you are fair. And I know that people have often taken advantage of your kindness. Due to the pain and disappointments you have endured, you built a wall around your heart to avoid further pain and disappointment.

I am encouraged concerning your deliverance from all of the hurt, pain, and discouragement because of the many people who have let you down, including me, because one of your favorite scriptures was Philippians 4:13: I can do all things through Christ who strengthens me. I believe in the God in you, and I am excited for your testimony because I know that it will be great!

I love you always, my sweet love. I know that our relationship is coming together each day!

Your name means "peaceful disposition." Take back your peace. Do not allow the devil to trick you out of your peace.

Love always and forever,
Mommy

My Prayer for Greg

Lord, I lift my son Greg up to you. I pray that you and your word are enough for Greg. You have given him a gift to grace the world with your words in an untraditional way. Satan is intimidated and would love to sift Greg as wheat, but thanks be unto God, every evil word spoken over Greg's life has been counted as canceled, in Jesus' name.

I pray that Greg serves you without restraints. Give him the strength and the strategy to execute every gift that you have anointed him with. Bless him with faith to be the father and husband that you have anointed him to be. I thank you, Lord, for Greg's relationship with you and for Greg's ability to reason with the truth of your word.

I thank you, God, for Greg's desire to love and protect his family. I thank you for Greg not allowing the negative words of others to dictate his life, nor to deter him from the path that you set before him. I thank you for Greg's ability to articulate his feelings and to advocate for himself and others. Greg will continue to stand up for the right. Thank you for the conviction of the Holy Ghost in Greg's life when he might be off course.

In Jesus' mighty name I pray. Amen.

Dear Gregory,

I love you, and I am so Godly proud of you! I love you, son, and I am honored to be you mother. I am proud to say that God has allowed us to be in each other's lives. It is an honor and a privilege to mother you!

You always said that you must protect and be there for your siblings. From the beginning, when people said negative things about you, I always knew that God made you different.

I often think about how hyper you were. But you are also so intelligent. Your first big word was "favorite," and I taught you how to read in twenty-five minutes.

Yes, you had challenges in elementary and middle schools, but in ninth grade, you started to do better in school. That was a new experience, and I know you struggled with the fear of the unknown. I know a lot of your motivation was to become a Marine—and also to get out of the house with my husband and me. I realize how miserable that he made it living there for you and your siblings who were here before the children that I had with him.

I know that you needed some things as a boy growing up, such as role models. I apologize that my previous decisions did not provide those options. I apologize that in our home you did not have a positive role model as a father. And yes from what was in place you learned how to survive. Thankfully for the men who came into your life, such as your coaches, your mentor, Jay O', and Craig, you were able to learn what the love of a father looked and felt like! And from our Father, God Himself!

I remember you came home one day in senior year and shared with me that one of your teachers mocked you about going to the Marines. I was pissed, and I wanted to confront her, but you begged me not to say anything to her. I remember saying, "I pray that God would deliver her to me," and He did. I got her. She watched her mouth from that point on. She never degraded my children after that. And she taught several of my children.

I know you had it tough after graduation with my ex-husband nitpicking with you over every little thing and placing me in a po-

135

sition to have to choose between you. But you did not allow that to stop you! You accomplished your goals getting your commercial drivers licenses and your apartment and being an involved father! You have so many great things ahead of you. Never stop believing in yourself!

You met your future wife, your beautiful baby boy was born in July 2019, and you received your Class A commercial driver's license (CDL) a few months after.

You have faced challenges, but God knows the path that He has set before you. No matter the detours, as long as you don't quit, you can't lose!

Even though you lacked a God-fearing father, you are an amazing father. You knew that you wanted something different for your son, and you are doing just that! Long before my children even though about having children, I always encouraged my sons to be active fathers and to love their children. Because of the lack from their own fathers, you are engaged in every aspect of your son's life!

I am so immensely proud of you!

I remember one of your favorite scriptures was Romans 7:21: "I find then a law, that when I would do good, evil is present with me."

Continue to keep God first and bask in what Jesus did on Calvary!

Gregory, your name means "watchful, vigilant." That is who you are: You believe in protecting our family!

Now just one last inside joke: Melatonin is not in my near future, and I will not be going to bed at 2000 hours.

Love always, my sweet boy,
Mama

Eric

When I found out I was pregnant with Eric, I was in a dark place in my life. I was depressed, and my self-esteem and self-worth were very low. At that time in my life, I was unaware of my value. This had been the case for many years before. However, at this stage of my life, things had really begin to weigh heavy on me. And I was pregnant with my fourth child and unbeknownst to me my third baby daddy. I had not faced the truth about my eldest child's father at that time.

I was drinking and smoking weed to cope. I was mentally unstable and emotionally broken.

During my pregnancy, I was living with Eric's father. I rode a rollercoaster of emotions. I was not mentally or emotionally mature at the time. But I gave it my best, with what I had to work with, during that time. Truth be told, I was unsure if I wanted to keep Eric. But after giving birth to him and seeing his sweet little face, those feelings went away.

My son Eric was the easiest birth that I had so far. In September 2000, I was watching the soaps *All My Children* and *One Life to Live* while I was delivering him!

Eric was a little bundle of joy, such a sweet little baby. He rarely cried. Because he was always smiling and winking his eyes, I nicknamed him "Winky."

Today, Eric is a father and an amazing provider for his two sons. He graduated high school on time and has an amazing work ethic. I am extremely proud of him, and I am grateful to be his mother!

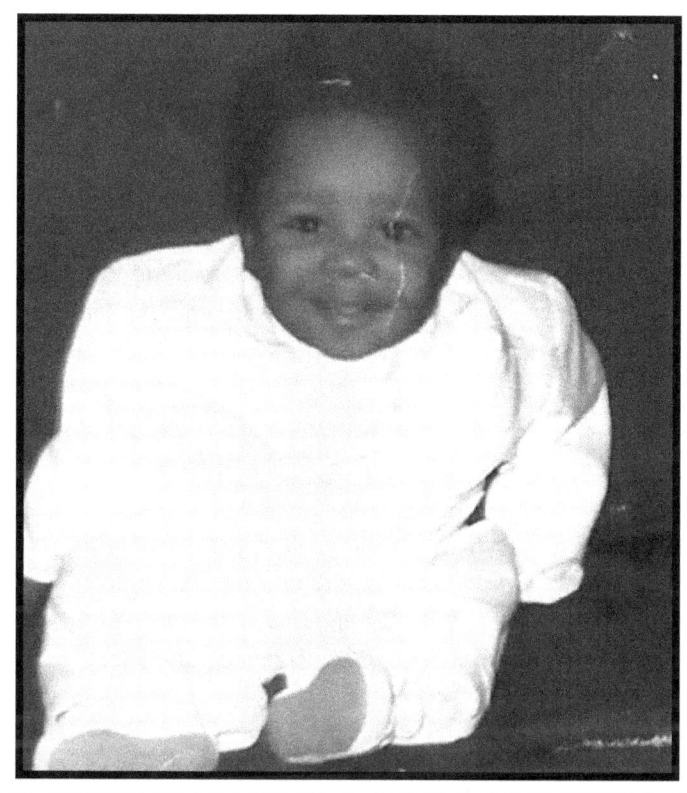

My Prayer for Eric

Father God, I lift Eric up to you, I thank you Lord for his life! I thank you, Lord God, for your forgiveness of his sins! I thank you, Lord God, for your keeping and sustaining power for Eric. I thank you, Lord God, for restoring his soul and placing him on a path of righteousness for your name.

Lord, thank you for never leaving nor forsaking Eric. I thank you, Lord, for the father that Eric is today and the brother, son, grandson, and friend.

Eric is loyal, and I pray, Lord, that you ready my son's heart for his future wife—a woman who respects him and prays with him through challenges and adversities. And he will love her as Christ loved the church!

Father, I pray that Eric would receive joy in place of the spirit of heaviness. Lord, I pray that you will heal his broken heart. I thank you, Lord God, for Eric's desires aligning with your will for his life. Please continue to show Eric your favor, grace, and mercy. In Jesus' mighty name. Amen.

Dear Eric,

Son, I know that you and I have had our battles over the years, but I am grateful that we have not allowed those things to stop us now in this season of life! I am so excited that you and I are back on speaking terms! I love you, and I am so proud of you!

I can still hear your little sweet voice singing, "Sometimes you have to encourage yourself." Always remember to encourage yourself, even when things appear to be at a standstill. Remember that God has not brought you this far to leave you now. God will always be a very present help in a time of trouble, and He will continue to help you.

You can do anything that you put your mind to. Do not let your past be an anchor. Remember that God has forgiven you for everything.

I remember that your favorite Scripture when we would have Bible study at home was 2ⁿᵈ Chronicles 7:14: "If my people, which are called by my name, shall humble themselves, and pray, and seek my face, and turn from their wicked ways: then will I hear from heaven and will forgive their sin, and heal their land." God is still the same God who desires to heal your land.

I believe in you, and I am excited for what God is about to do in your life! Continue to press because your two little ones need you!

Eric, you were named after me. Your name means "sole ruler" or better "eternal ruler." Walk in who God has positioned you to be. Thank you for forgiving me!

Love always,
Mama

Arabia

Just a few days before my mama's birthday in August 2004, I gave birth to my sweet baby girl Arabia. It was scary because as my contractions were intensifying, my baby's heart rate continued to drop. The umbilical cord was wrapped around her neck, and I had to have an emergency C-section. Prior to that, I remember her father saying no one except him could be in the room while I was giving birth to her, but I was used to having family with me with all of my births. Well that didn't work out too good for him because we were not married yet, and he ended up not being able to see her born either. God has a way of showing us that we are not running anything!

Another strange thing during the course of the delivery was one of my family members singing "I'm Going Up Yonder." She was corrected by her mother. I often think about that, especially since at that time this became an emergency labor. Maybe Arabia's daddy was on to something. Despite all that occurred, everything turned out okay with my baby and me!

Arabia's father recorded me after I had Arabia, and I observed some things in the video. The nurse cross-contaminated, using the same gloves to touch items in the room then coming back and touching my incision. I was too out of it to advocate for myself, and I know that Arabia's dad did not know any better. But God!

As Arabia was growing up and blossoming into an amazing, anointed little being, I became concerned. She would not talk, even around two years old. I took her to Cincinnati Children's Hospital's speech department, where Arabia learned sign

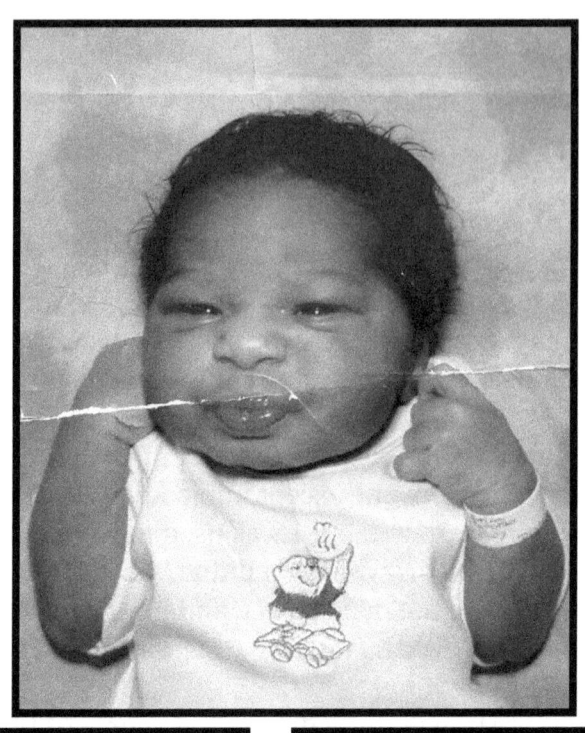

language. I was devastated that my baby could not talk. All she would do is stare at me.

I later learned that Arabia could talk all along; she just did not want to talk at the time! She is smart as a whip. Once Arabia began to talk, she brought correction, wisdom, and knowledge to our family! Her middle name means "the Lord is here." Arabia has always been very bright, and she loves to learn, I breast fed her the longest; she hates it when I tell her she just would not get off the breast! It paid off!

The only trouble that I have out of Arabia is she does not like to wash the dishes, and one time in school a boy was bothering her in the first grade and she tried to glue him to the chair with some Elmer's glue! Her teacher told me, "I didn't want the other children to see me laughing, but I *felt* Arabia. That kid won't sit still." end quote.

Everywhere Arabia goes, she is loved. People gravitate toward her. She is tiny but mighty. She lives up to her name and knows that everywhere she goes, the Lord is with her! She is beautiful, smart, and kind.

Once she said to me, "I am not being disrespectful; however, I am not like you and Camisha and Serenity." At first, I was offended, but quickly the Lord checked me because she was absolutely right, finally the curse was broken! Arabia is neither haughty nor arrogant. She is aware of who she is in Christ Jesus, and I see her continuing to grow in the grace of God.

All throughout Arabia's school career, she has taken her education seriously, now my baby has a full scholarship at Ohio State University. I am extremely proud of her! She is doing it in Jesus' name. She will make it to the finish line and beyond!

My Prayer for Arabia

Lord, I lift Arabia up to you. Oh God! I come against the spirit of fear and anxiety. I thank you, Oh God, for providing all of her needs according to your riches in Glory. Father God, thank you for ordering Arabia's steps and protecting her from all hurt, harm, and danger.

Thank you, merciful Father God, for blessing me with this beautiful vessel. Thank you for allowing me to parent her, walk with her, and love her. Thank you, Jesus!

I thank you in advance, Oh God, for giving Arabia her heart's desires that are within Your will for her life!

I thank you, Oh God, for your continued grace and mercy toward Arabia, and I cancel every evil word, which comes from a place of jealousy over my baby's life spoken by the enemy, in the name of Jesus. Lord, I thank you for Arabia's continued provision.

Thank you, Oh God, for the many people who have come together to help my baby while she has been in school. Bless them and their families and everything that they stand in the need of.

I thank you, Lord, that Arabia's faith will continue to grow as she sees You provide for her and work situations out for her. Thank you, Oh God, that she will recall her history with you, and she knows that You change not. You are a God of consistency, continue to let her know that she can trust You and take You at your word. I thank you, Oh God, for the excellent wife and mother that Arabia will be. I ask all of these things in Jesus' mighty mame. Amen.

Dear Arabia,

Girl, where do I start? You just tell it like it is! Sometimes it is like you are my mama! You encourage me, and to be honest I look up to you! Never stop being you and continue to allow God to be your guiding force. You are a leader, a true force to be reckoned with! I see you operating in your field that God has purposed you for! You are going to be an asset no matter where God takes you! Continue to take a stand for what is right! Keep the Lord first, and you will never lose!

Mommy is so Godly proud of you. I know that you do not like all of the attention. I am proud because to be honest, me and all of my children have been written off, but the devil keeps getting smacked down. Continue to keep your foot on his neck. I know that we do not always agree, but I love how we come back together.

Suga, you all give me a reason to live! And as long as I have breath in my body, I will be her for y'all! I am so glad that I gave y'all Jesus. Stay close to Him!

Thank you for your favorite scripture, James 1:19: "My dear brothers and sisters, take note of this: Everyone should be quick to listen, slow to speak, and slow to become angry." (NIV) I have gotten better, but I have a way to go!

As stated earlier, Arabia, you brought correction to the family. I remember you telling Camisha to be obedient when we lived on Elkton Place. And she listened to you. I often wonder when you were not talking at first, was it because you were checking us out? You were living out that Scripture long before you even knew what it was!

Arabia means "she knows," and your middle name Shammah means "the Lord is here." Keep living out your name and purpose! Oh yes and pack light, girl. You need a U-Haul for real. Thank God I know how to pack stuff, or none of your things would fit!

Love always,
Mommy

DJ

Another easy labor, DJ was born in April 2006, such a wonderful little bundle of joy! He gave me another reason to keep living! His birth was so easygoing that I was able to deliver him naturally, with no complications whatsoever!

During his pregnancy, I thought, *Finally, I can say that I gave birth to a baby while I was married.* DJ was not born under the curse of me having babies out of wedlock.

I was actually baptized as an adult while I was pregnant with DJ—by water and slain in the Holy Ghost with the edification of speaking in tongues. This was huge for me! I dedicated all of my children back to God at birth. DJ though got it all while he was still in my womb. This was different, and you could tell DJ's demeanor was different.

Unfortunately, Satan had plans for my baby. As he began to grow up as a little boy, he was injured a lot. He had to have stitches several times. He was always getting hurt, especially head injuries. The devil is a liar. Satan, you can NOT have my baby. DJ also has a severe food allergy.

DJ and I have had our difficulties, but we absolutely love each other. He is very compassionate and loving. He is willing to understand things from another person's point of view. He loves his siblings! But of course, they all love each other! I raised my children to stick together!

DJ recently graduated from high school—my sixth child to graduate! I am blessed to be his mother.

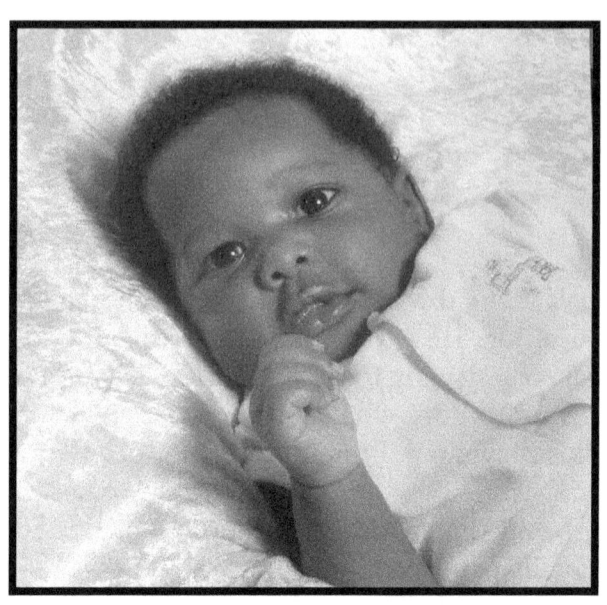

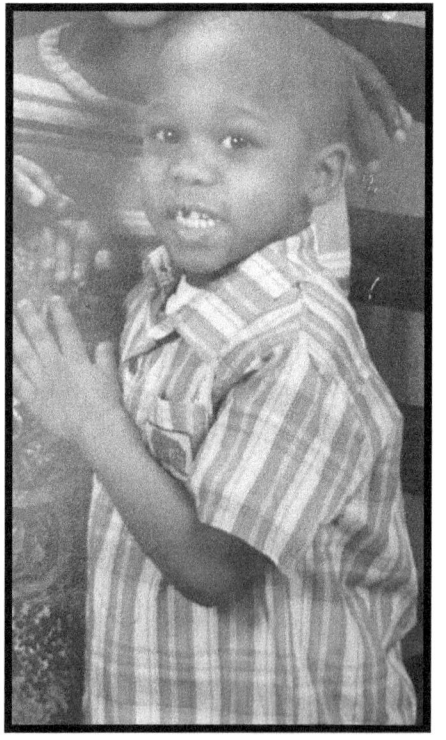

My Prayer for DJ

Lord, I come to you and ask for your continued protection over DJ. Lord God, I thank you for your continued grace and mercy over DJ's life. Thank you, Lord, for your warring angels who are encamped around about him. Guard DJ's mind, Oh Lord, against any neurological issues from all of the head injuries. Father God, order his steps and cause him to desire you and your will for his life.

I thank you, Lord God, for DJ's bright beautiful future, despite his past decisions. I stand in agreement with DJ concerning his future and all that he desires to accomplish! I thank you, God, for favor concerning DJ and for the change that is still taking place in DJ's life. In Jesus' mighty name I pray. Amen.

Dear DJ,

I want to start by saying that I love you! I am so proud of you! I know that you can make it, and if I have breath in my body, I am here for you! I want you to be self-sufficient, only depend on God and yourself. Be a man of integrity; be a man of your own word. Stand for something, Son, or you will fall for anything.

I know that you did not believe that I would send you back to Cincinnati. Just knowing that I have not given up on you. I saw some things afar off, and I had to stop them before they manifested. When you come back, you will be ready for the blessings that God has set up here for you in North Carolina. You will be able to have experience enough to share with your children one day, which will teach them responsibility and discipline. Simple acts like holding the door open for people and respecting people, honoring them with the fear of the Lord.

You will be able to teach your children what it means to value a warning and to take people at their word. You have had to learn some extremely hard lessons—early, But I believe that because of the call of God on your life, those things were necessary for your growth and relationship with Christ!

God anointed you before you even got here on this Earth, He allowed me to carry greatness on the inside of me, and He covered you while on the inside of me. I believe that is why Satan tried his hardest to destroy you with all of the head injuries.

Do not give up on yourself and do not worry about the negative words of ignorant people. Press forward and go by what God has spoken of your life. Continue to focus on this Scripture that the Lord gave you, Galatians 6:4: "Pay careful attention to your own work, for then you will get the satisfaction of a job well done, and you won't need to compare yourself to anyone else's."

Stick with this, Son, and life will be easy because each day that God graces you to see will be an adventure for something new for you to experience in your relationship with God, the creator of the universe. You will be able to see how He carries you from day to day and appreciate His great love for you and the magnitude of His mercies that are everlasting!

Dwight, your name means "devoted follower." If you give your devotion to God, everything else will fall in place! I love you, and I am excited for the next chapter of your life!

Love always,
Ma Dukes J

Amoz

Lord has mercy! This boy right here, born in June 2008, I mean to tell you he kept me running, and I mean literally. I thought that I was going to be able to deliver him naturally, but my doctor saw the pain that I was in and asked? "Why don't you go ahead and get an epidural before it is too late, so that you are not uncomfortable?" I am glad that I did!

Once Amoz was born, he was one of the most precious little beings. He had cool-black hair, which was full and came down his neck. Oh my God I just adored this boy, and so did his daddy. The baby came before me!

Amoz grew up and started to walk, then run. I was so nervous because I used to worry that he would run into the street. He was a busy little boy, and he could run fast, and he thought it was funny to have me chasing him around. It was not funny to me, but what he did not know is that he was too sweet for me to whip him.

Amoz's first word was when he called his sister "Mooda." He was always laughing, such a happy, energetic baby! But sometimes I feel like the laughter was a part of him being mischievous.

When Amoz got older, all the running paid off, he had speed, and it played a positive role for him in sports. The boy is quick on his feet. And thankfully, he got older, and was not as mischievous, as he was as a little tot. Because he is a handsome young man, athletic and physically built, the little girls are his issue. The rest of my sons are handsome young men and extremely attractive as well. I just see that I must stay on Amoz more than my other sons about these gals.

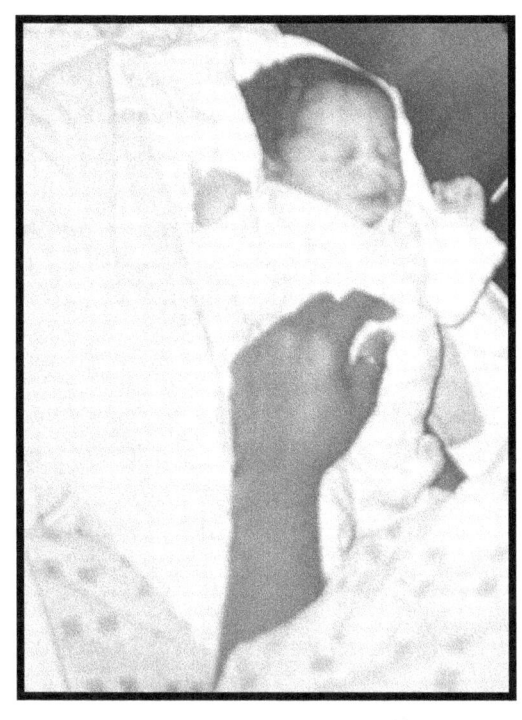

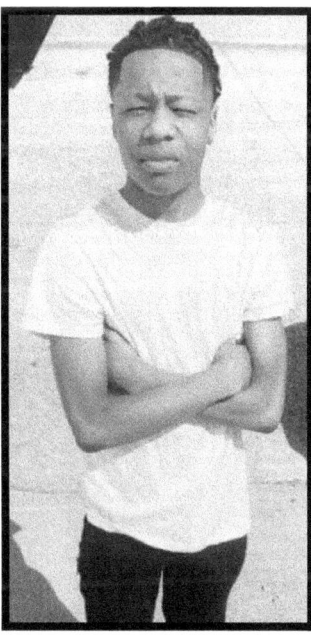

He is highly intelligent and will advocate for himself. But I have to say that every one of my children will advocate for themselves. Though I am not surprised because they are my children! I am just saying! As Amoz has grown up, he amazes me because of how chill he is now and how loving he is. I know that he loves me, and I certainly love him! He is not a mama's boy, which would be Greg and Joshua! I had to laugh, just thinking about how all my other children talk about those two!

My Prayer for Amoz

Lord, I come to you asking you to bless Amoz from the crown of his head to the very soles of his feet. I plead the blood of Jesus Christ over my son, and Lord, I thank you for his life.

Lord, I thank you for Amoz accomplishing every goal that he has ever imagined, and I thank you, Lord, for Amoz's desire to get to know you on a deeper level. I thank you, Lord, for Amoz sending me Scriptures and encouraging me in the Lord. I thank you, Lord, that Amoz will save himself for one woman and that he will desire to be a god-fearing husband and father. Lord, I thank you for allowing Amoz to take learning seriously, and that Amoz will always look forward to learning new things. Lord never allow Amoz to place limits on you or on himself. I pray, Lord God, that Amoz will use all his gifts and talents to bring your name glory. I pray that Amoz will no longer stutter. Allow this thing that appears to be a disability to cause Amoz to think before he speaks so all his words will be full of wisdom and mercy. Lord, I ask all these things in the mighty name of Jesus. Amen.

Dear Amoz,

I want to start by saying that I love you! I am extremely proud of you! You have developed into a fine young man, and you have a beautiful spirit!

I see you going far in this life, never give up on yourself, and always dream big! Remember that everything that you desire that is within God's will for your life, right at your fingertips. You have everything that you need to be successful.

I know that I held you back in school. If you ever question why, it was because I knew that you needed a little more time. Sometimes in life we must do things a few times before we get it! And really that is okay. The timetable that God has set for your life is right on schedule where He wants you to be. Please be encouraged in this because it will alleviate any doubts that you may have concerning how things are going for you at this time. Also, during this next phase of your life you will have a deeper level of appreciation, for the blessings that God places before you!

Amoz, your name means "strong increaser." Continue to live up to your name! And only follow Jesus, not the crowd! In this season, I had to make the decision to send you with your daddy. Make the best of it. Do the right thing, and the right thing will follow you.

Love always,
Momma

Joshua

The last of my tribe of eight, born in December 2010! This was one of the hardest labors; this boy like to have killed me. He was seven pounds and fourteen ounces. I gave birth to Joshua naturally. During that process, my body went through more trauma than I had have ever experienced in any of my children that I gave birth to, and I have had some very eventful labors, to say the least. But Joshua and I both were determined for him to be here.

Once I delivered my beautiful baby boy, I was so tired. I could not push anymore, so that the placenta could come out. I was given some pain medication once I delivered and allowed a few minutes to rest.

Unbeknownst to me, I was hemorrhaging behind the placenta. My doctor said to me, "Erica, I need you to push this out or I'm going to have to pull it out." I said, "Do what you have to do. I am tired." Why did I say that? My doctor began to peel the placenta from my uterine walls, now that was excruciatingly painful! As he was pulling down, I was crawling backward up the bed. What I realized is, it was necessary for my doctor to remove the placenta, or I could have died.

There are times when there are things in our lives that are hidden and there can be hemorrhaging in our lives that can cause death of potential, death of purpose, death of relationships, and death of opportunities, if they are not peeled back and exposed. Our own hidden agendas can cause death if we are not careful to be honest with our own selves! Nevertheless, Joshua and I made it! He was healthy and strong, full of life, and naturally my baby had a love for the Lord! And he still does!

My Prayer for Joshua

Lord God, I bring Joshua before you, I pray, Lord, that Joshua will never lose his fire for you! I pray, merciful Father, That Joshua knows that he is loved, and that his life is valuable!

I come against the spirit of suicide. I thank you, Lord, for Joshua being a change agent at this early age. I pray to the Lord that Joshua knows that he has been set apart for such a time as this.

I thank you, Oh Gracious God, that Joshua will forever identify with you as His primary source of life. Lord, I thank you for Joshua's bright future in you and the many victories that you have set before him, be made known to his subconscious mind.

Lord, order Joshua's steps to run toward you, and you only with direction for his life.

I thank you in advance, Oh God, for the husband and father that he will be, to raise his own children in the fear and admonition of the Lord. I thank you, Lord God, for Joshua's leadership! I pray that Joshua has a desire to learn and to seek you first in everything that he does!

In Jesus' name, I pray. Amen.

Dear Joshua,

Baby, I love you. I know that this season is painful, but what I want you to know is that God knows best, and He will never make any mistakes. He is faithful and true, and He will never lie. You can depend on him!

I really do miss you and your brothers! In this season though God is allowing you all to see and learn some lessons. And spend some more time with you all's daddy! Often things may appear to be worse than it really is, just remember things have a way of always working out! And I am always going to be around as, long as God has breath in my body!

Even when my time is up, always remember that I told you and your sisters and brothers that God comes before me, and He will never leave you! You can bet your last dollar that the only way that I will not be around is if God has called me home! Nothing will ever make me stop loving any of you!

It is truly an honor and a privilege for me to mother all eight of you all! Always remember that you can tell me anything. I will not judge you. You can trust me. If not, trust the God in me! I believe in you, baby, and I am excited to see your future. I know that it is going to be amazing! Keep your hand in the hands of God, and you will not lose! I love you Always my Joking!

Love Always,

Mama

Erica Anderson

Dear Mama,

Although you are not here with me, I want you to know that I miss you. There are many days that I wish that I could just hold you in my arms and love you the way that you deserved.

I know that I apologized before God took you away from me. What I want to do for the rest of my days is please God and restore your brokeness, by helping other women who may suffer from addiction, low self-worth, domestic abuse, and loneliness. Leading them to the one who can fill every void and restore their joy.

I never got the closure that I needed. I was your only baby, and I needed you so much. What I realize now is that you were hurting, and you did not know how to even love yourself.

Thank you for not aborting me, I love you! And I have forgiven you!

Love,
Erica

Celebrating the Life

Of

Ms. Linda Burch

Funeral Service

Thursday, May 23, 2002 – 7:00 p.m.

Dear Daddy,

I know that you are not here with me. When you were in the hospital, and I was at your bedside, the only thing that I could get out was how you were not there for me and how I was here for you at that time. There was so much more I wanted to say, but the truth of the matter is that was all that really needed to be said at that moment. I forgive you.

I don't know what it was that kept you from showing me love and affection. My scars run so deep. I can remember on several Christmas's, how I would get your stepson's toys instead of what was for me. I always felt like our time was rushed, and the mix up in the Christmas gifts showed it. Even when you came to visit me when you were released from jail.

When my mama died, I needed you so bad, but even then, you visited me for a short time. It was like I was in your way.

So I sought out love in boys who were in grown bodies. The unfortunate part is they treated me just how you treated women, like an object.

I loved you so much. I believed in you. You broke my heart into millions of little pieces. When counterfeit love showed up, I was moved because LOVE and ATTENTION are what I desired most from you. I wonder had you only given me that, how my life would have been so different.

I choose to forgive you, because there is nothing we can do to change it now. And to top that off, I have come to really know the FATHER'S love on a grander scale. He LOVED me so much that He sent HIS only begotten son to die for me!

Sincerely,
Erica

HOMEGOING SERVICE

Paul Douglas Anderson
October 29, 1958—June 9, 2012

TURDAY, JUNE 16, 2012-11:00 AM

ist Emmanuel Christian Fellowship

2324 May Street

Cincinnati, OH 45206

Bishop Michael Dantley

Erica Anderson

If you have children of your own or someone who is near and dear to your heart, take this time to write a letter to them.

_____

_____

_____

_____

_____

_____

_____

_____

_____

_____

_____

_____

_____

_____

_____

_____

_____

_____

_____

Acknowledgments

I would like to thank God for giving me the grace to get through this. This was not easy but with the help of the Lord I was able to finish!

Thank you my love, John when I needed you to listen to me read aloud, even though you were tired, and you did not judge me. You asked me hard questions and caused me to really think. I love you!

Thanks to my children, even though y'all were busy, y'all each took time to hear from me concerning this book. I really appreciate y'all's feedback. I love each of you!

Thank you to my Bishop Michael E. Dantley and Pastor Carol B. Dantley. Being a member at Christ Emmanuel Christian Fellowship in Cincinnati, Ohio, and serving in the capacity in which I did has prepared me for the rest of my life. I am so very grateful for my Bishop and Pastor for the teachings that came across the pulpit and in those classrooms that was and is the word of the Living God. I would not be the person who I am today, in my faith in God had it not been for the both of you!

Thank you, Aunt Rachel, for encouraging me over the years to share my story! I love you and thank you for believing in me and encouraging me in the Lord!

Thank you, Aunt Marietta, for listening to me, when I needed a listening ear. Thank you, Pammy, for encouraging me to get finished, Sis! And thank you to the man and woman of God Pastor Jeremy and Pastor Sosa from "One Place Church" thank you for being obedient to God with preaching the word of God, when I was ready to throw in the towel. God spoke through you, and it allowed me to finish strong!

I would like to thank everyone who over the years did not believe in me. You pushed me closer to the Lord! Those situations that were set in place to destroy me were steppingstones to my destiny. I forgive you.

"You prepare a table before me in the presence of my enemies.
You have anointed and refreshed my head with oil;
My cup overflows."
—Psalm 23:5

About the Author

Erica Renee Anderson was born and raised in Cincinnati, Ohio. A mother of eight children and grandmother of eight grandchildren, Erica has been in the medical field since 1996. She has been a nurse for eleven-and-a-half years. Erica has also been an ordained minister since 2015. Erica is the owner and operator of The Least of These Home Health LLC and Intentional Means LLC. Her main objective is to see people whole and living out the ordained purpose that God Almighty created them for. Erica loves nature and finds great joy spending time outdoors and near big bodies of water, listening to the peaceful sound of the wind against the water!

"For I know the thoughts that I think towards you," saith the Lord, "thoughts of peace, and not of evil, to give you an expected end."
—Jeremiah 29:11 (KJV)

www.ingramcontent.com/pod-product-compliance
Lightning Source LLC
Chambersburg PA
CBHW061757120626
46550CB00005B/2036